THE PINE ISLAND INCIDENT

JEFF HARDING

HANGAR 1 PUBLISHING

CONTENTS

1

"THE INVITE"

A famous naturalist named Aldo Leupold once said, "There are some who can live without wild things, and some who can not." I grew up with a clear understanding that I was one of those who could not. As the son of a hunting guide, I was introduced to more than just the outdoors. I learned what the wilderness looked like. Those areas of the world that are reserved for only those who had a knowledge of how to survive them. My father had that type of knowledge, and he had a passion for making sure he passed it on to me. By the time I was in high school, I had already experienced what it was like to be in truly remote areas while hunting elk, bear and other large game in Wyoming, Montana, and Idaho. My father taught me the hard lessons of how to resist the panic of being lost, or how to find the calm while things were coming apart around you. He helped me unlock the secret of showing reverence to a landscape that can choose to reveal its most beautiful features or swallow you whole.

As a student, I often found myself daydreaming of higher adventures than a classroom could afford. My grades were average at best. I was not going to receive any college scholarships for my academic accomplishments, I really didn't have any. I enjoyed sports but did not perform at a level worthy of a free ride anywhere. So, naturally, when the Army recruiter came strolling the hallways at my high school, my curiosity had me in pursuit. After some testing and a few physical exams, I was guaranteed a college tuition package and a spot in the US Army's EOD school. The Bomb Squad. I graduated the last week in May 1987, and I would be leaving for Basic Training at the end of July. I had about 6 weeks to fit a whole summer into before I had to leave.

While at one of my best friend's graduation parties, he mentioned to me that he, his little brother, his father, and several of his uncles and cousins were leaving on a fishing trip in Canada and asked if I'd like to join them. The trip was going to be fishing for 8 days at a very remote location 120 miles northeast of Flin Flon, Manitoba. The lake was Granville Lake, part of the Churchill Reservoir system and would take us over 20 hours to drive the 1,000-plus miles to get there. I told my parents about the offer, and they agreed it would be a great opportunity to go on an adventure before having to leave for the Army. I was excited. I'd been to a lot of areas hunting and fishing, but never that far north in Canada.

My friend Todd was a lot like me. We both excelled in the outdoors and his father was also an avid outdoorsman who had passed on so many experiences to his sons. Todd and I were both 18 and his younger brother Jamie had just turned 14. We were the only "kids" on this trip as all of his cousins and uncles were in their late 20s and older. Although all three of us were capable, our age placed us in a position where we felt this was an opportunity to show them that we were their equals when it came to outdoorsmanship. For me, with my life's next chapter about to start on an Explosive Ordinance Disposal team in the US Army, it was also a chance to prove to myself that I was ready for such an endeavor.

Todd and I were cut from the same cloth. We both were outgoing in school and our friends would describe us both as outgoing and maybe even popular. I didn't know his little brother Jamie that well. Jamie was the youngest of four brothers and he was quiet. I don't think he would be the type anyone would consider popular, mostly because he seemed shy if you didn't know him well. He was the type that would smile at a joke instead of laugh at it. Todd was the levelheaded one. He wasn't animated and hardly ever showed concern or worry. While everyone else would think out loud, he was always the one taking it all in, measuring options, calculating risks, and doing it quietly. If he was ever excited or nervous, he never showed it on the outside. I appreciated this about him. If you ever needed a straight answer with no BS, he could deliver it unfiltered with a calmness that made you feel his advice was solid.

2

"ONWARD"

We left on a Thursday. I drove to Todd's house and left my vehicle there as I joined his family. There were 10 of us. Todd, Jamie and I, his dad, three uncles and three cousins. We would take two vehicles. One was a Ford F250 pulling a large livestock trailer that had five 16-foot aluminum boats piled into the back of it with five 25-horse outboard motors. The other was a Chevy Suburban. Todd, Jamie, and I were in the truck with his dad and one of his uncles. The first leg of the journey brought us to Fargo ND and it took 5 hours to get there. It was an excruciating five hours because Todd's dad and his uncle listened to old country western music full blast. Occasionally there would be a song we all would sing out loud but for the most part, we wore our Walkman and headphones in the back seat. When we stopped for gas, I was standing outside of the trailer looking through the slats at the boats. It looked like there was room in there for a couple teenage boys. I'm not sure in today's era of road safety we could have pulled this off, but we asked his dad if we could ride back there. I think at first, he agreed because he figured that within a few miles, we would decide it was a bad idea and beg to come back up front in the truck.

250 miles later, we stopped for fuel again. Todd, Jamie, and I were having a ball back there. We had turned one of the boats over upside right and were "riding in it" like we were out on the lake. His dad made us move up into the truck because we were about to cross the border and there was a border checkpoint where they did an inspection. At the checkpoint, I was amazed to find out that the Canadian Mounties look just like they did in the cartoons. Their red coats and black hats were bustling around the two vehicles and looking in the trailer. They asked us what our purpose for the trip was, where we were going etc. They asked Paul's dad if they had any beer or alcohol with them. The adults in our party were big fans of beer and had brought about 15 cases with them. I thought it looked like they were going to be there for a month instead of ten days when I saw all the cases of beer laid out in the parking lot in a row. The Mounties explained that each person of age was allowed one case of beer. There were seven adults in the group over 21. For the other cases, we would have to pay a tax of $36 per case to bring with us, or we could leave them there. The Mounties asked Todd and I how old we were, and we answered 18 and showed our drives licenses. The Mounties moved two more cases into the keeper pile. Todd looked at me with huge eyes and as it turns out, in Canada, you can drink if you are over 18!

It was decided we would drive from the inspection point to a local restaurant. It was a small-town café on the main street in a little town I can't remember the name of. The waitress came over and took our lunch orders as we all sat at two large tables.

She asked me, "What would you like to drink?"

I smiled at her and asked, "Do you serve beer here?"

Todd and I sat there and ate our cheeseburgers with a tall glass of cold beer. His dad just shook his head at us like he wanted to comment but knew it was a well-played effort on our part.

We got back in the trailer and drove another few hundred miles into the evening. I thought we would be stopping at a hotel, but I was wrong. Todd's uncles and cousins just kept rotating drivers and we were going to drive it straight through. By morning we eventually reached the old logging town of Flin Flon. It sat on the Manitoba side of the Manitoba/Saskatchewan border. We felt we were getting close. By the map, it looked as if we were only about 120 miles from our destination.

As we stood outside of a gas station we had fueled up at, we noticed a small sporting goods store and tackle shop. We walked over to check it out. It was run by an old man who was a local First Nations Inuit who was very nice, and talkative but apparently not good at math. I decided to buy a new fishing reel. It was a high-end Shimano reel that had a handwritten price tag that said $72. It was expensive but I felt like there weren't going to be many places a person could spend money at from here on out and I had taken a couple hundred dollars with me on the trip.

He looked at the price tag and rang it up and said, "That will be $27, young man."

I replied, "I'll take two of them."

I sat in the back of that trailer putting a new line on the pair of reels while Todd gave me grief on how he felt I took advantage of the man. He didn't have to say it, I was already feeling it and inside I was regretting it. In that moment, I found myself doing some self-examination and realized that one of the things I admired about Todd was that he had scruples. To him, there was never a right time to do the wrong thing. And that realization had me feeling awful. I decided that on the way home, Id ask Todd's dad to stop at the store and I would pay the store owner the difference.

3

"THE ARRIVAL"

That last 120 miles ended up being more than anyone of us were prepared for. They weren't paved roads or even gravel roads. They were more like tank trails that veered wildly through the woods and between the lakes. We couldn't ride in the trailer for fear of suffering a concussion. The roads had giant potholes and rotted logs across them. We made our way onward and ended up arriving at the remote camp about 8 hours later. It was starting to get dark, but we had time to look at the area and took it all in.

I was aware we were going to an off-the-grid primitive area and would be sleeping in tents, but once we stood at the lake and looked out across it, it was surreal just how far off the grid we had gone. The lake was huge. It was dotted with islands and surrounded on every shoreline by tall pines, poplars, birch, and cedar. There were no cabins anywhere, no boats on the water and no apparent civilization anywhere. No power lines on the horizon and no lights anywhere. The camp was run by three brothers who were in their 50s and 60s. They were also Inuit First Nations people and Todd's dad knew them from a pat hunting trip he was on there years ago. Their faces were weathered, and they lived there year-round. They had a small cabin, and they guided a few fishermen in the summer but mainly made a living guiding moose hunter in the fall. They ran trap lines in the winter and had furs and traps hanging all over. There was a picnic shelter area by a large campfire pit and there was a fire going. By the lake's edge, there were two docks and a small run-down boat house that looked to be used for storage with old traps and canoe paddles hanging all over the outside of it.

The tents we would sleep in were already set up and Todd, Jamie, and I would have our own tent away from the others. Todd and I moved our bags and gear into the tent. We laid out sleeping bags and got the lantern ready to light up later once it was completely dark. I could sense the excitement in Todd and Jamie's eyes as we all anticipated what the coming days would bring.

We sat out by the fire with the rest of the adults and heard the guides talk about the fishing and what we could expect. The lake didn't get much pressure from anyone else and catching limits of Walleye, Northern Pike and Lake Trout were common. They shared with us their knowledge of what tackle and lures to use. They were adamant about us understanding how easy it is to get lost on the lake. They gave us laminated lake maps that showed the camp location and a depth map of the entire lake. The map showed several islands scattered around the lake and since they were all wooded and higher in elevation than the water level, it would be easy to be on the back side of an island and not see the camp area. It's disorienting and getting lost is easy. They gave us a few small walkie-talkie-type radios. You must remember that this was 1987, there were no smartphones or GPS. They said if we got lost to stay put and they would eventually come and find us. We would fish in the morning hours and come into camp mid-day for lunch and then fish the second half of the day. During these breaks, we would explain to the guide hosts and the rest of the party what area each boat intended to fish.

After a few hours of listening to their instructions and a few stories, Todd, Jamie, and I made our way to the tent. We all were asleep quick as it had been a lot of driving, and this was the first time to really lay flat and stretch out.

4

"THE ROUTINE"

When I woke up, I could still smell the campfire smoke in the air, but it was much colder. It was the first week in June and there was frost on everything outside. We dressed warmly in jeans and layered t-shirts under long sleeve thermal shirts and hoodies. Todd and I had gotten the campfire going again and Jamie was still asleep. The other adults were also still in their tents, and it was quiet. Todd and I started to unload the outboard motors, gas tanks, oars, life jackets, etc. Once his cousins were awake, we all unloaded the boats and brought them to the docks. We rigged the motors and got them each started, making sure each ran smoothly. The guides made a breakfast of eggs, bacon, hash browns and coffee. Everyone sat down around the fire and ate. I took my plate and a bottle of water down to the dock and sat at the water's edge. It was quiet. The water was smooth and as you looked out across it you couldn't see the islands or the opposite shore as the morning fog lay across the water. The temp had risen to above freezing and everything just felt damp. A few hundred yards from the dock there was a loon sitting still on the water and you could hear it calling out every few minutes. I could see it on the edge of the fog and it would dive under. After a minute or so it would pop up far away from where it disappeared. There wasn't anything special about the eggs or the bacon. I'm not even sure if they were real eggs, that may have been the best breakfast I've ever had to this day. It occurred to me that prior to that morning, every time I had been in the wilderness, there were likely other hunters within ten miles of me, probably closer. But right now, other than the guys sitting around that fire, there likely wasn't anyone within 50 miles or more of where we were. This was the most remote area I had ever been to.

Todd and his brother got in the boat, and I grabbed my fishing rods and tackle box off the table by the fire and got in the boat too. Todd ran the motor as I looked at the map sitting in front of him on the middle seat. Jamie sat in the front of the boat and his dad stood on the dock and gave us the fatherly warning not to do anything stupid. Don't go too far out on the first day. Just work on getting our feet under us and used to the area. As we pulled away from the dock, I asked Todd where we wanted to go to start fishing and he said he would let me choose. We spent most of the morning just a mile down the shore by one of the islands. We cast for Northern Pike and Walleye up in the shallows of a point. We had caught fish on almost every cast. It was amazing and the three of us thought there was no way those other guys were out fishing us. We kept several of each species on a stringer thinking it would be up to us to feed everyone since we were the best in the world at catching these fish. At noon, we headed back to camp and as we pulled up to the dock, the others were there, and we were grinning ear to ear. Jamie held up our stringer and they were pointing at us and we sat proud in that boat in full hero mode. As we tied off the boat, we started telling them all our war stories of reeling in the big ones, how we caught them almost every cast. Then we watched each of them grab their full stringers and carry them to the fish cleaning table and we were instantly humbled by the realization that we had only tied for the best in the world at catching them. But we held our own and we reveled in the idea that we had kept the pace. After lunch, we headed back out and released everything we caught, which were quite a few. When we arrived at the dock that evening, Todd's dad asked if we had kept any fish. Jamie told him, "We release all the big ones and that's all we caught were big ones." Touché'.

That evening around the fire we heard the other guys talking about seeing a moose swimming in the lake and they had pulled up next to it while it swam. I had seen deer, moose, and even bear swimming in lakes in Northern Minnesota. Jamie hadn't seen that before and said he was hoping he would see it while we were there. That night around the fire, we heard wolves howling across the lake. It sounded like there were dozens of them in different areas. The sound carried so clearly, and it sounded as if they were closer than they probably were. Regardless, we didn't fall asleep as easily that night. About every hour or two they would sound off and start howling again.

The next morning, we ate breakfast and headed out fishing again. This time we got a little braver as we ventured further out and further down the shoreline. We were careful to note on the map where each island was as we rounded it out of the sightline of camp. Every foot of shoreline looked similar to all the rest. There were no significant landmarks, no cabins, or clearings. It was a solid timber shoreline as far as you could see. After fishing for a few hours, we decided to troll our way back to the camp using crankbaits. Jamie jumped up to the front of the boat and was pointing as Todd and I looked and saw it. A cow moose and a year-ling swimming in the water. They were between an island and the main shore crossing a narrow channel about a ½ mile wide. We trolled up near them and we watched them making sure we kept enough distance not to make them nervous. Jamie was ecstatic that he was seeing this. He was grinning and just in awe that we were getting to see this so close. Eventually, we reeled in and took off toward camp. When we got back, Jamie spent an hour telling everyone what we had seen.

That afternoon was much like the one before. We caught a lot of fish and we released them all. We had pulled the boat up on the main shore on a sandy beach and just sat around on shore as the temp was close to 75 degrees. It was crazy how the temps would be cold in the morning and by mid-afternoon you would be wearing shorts and a t-shirt. We even jumped in the water and swam for a bit, but it was chilly. The water was so clear, and you could easily see the bottom at 15 feet deep. As we got in the boat, we decided to stop every time we saw a decent drop-off close to shore and take a few casts before moving on.

We were all three casting at a shoreline and catching nice walleyes every few casts. Jamie had turned around quickly to look at a fish that his brother had caught and in doing so he hit his rod with his leg and over the edge it went. It sunk quickly to the bottom, and we looked over the edge and could see it laying there on the bottom. Jamie was upset and worried about what his dad would say when he found out he lost it. I told him to not worry, we can get it. I tried to snag it with a casting spoon with a treble hook, but it didn't work. It was frustrating to see it so clearly just laying there on the bottom. I took off my shirt, my shorts and in my underwear, I jumped in the lake and swam down to the bottom and got it. I was freezing to the point I was turning blue. But we were close to camp so it would be a quick ride back.

I got out of the boat in my underwear and walked down the dock without saying a word as the others just stared wondering what the hell.... Finally, Todd's dad snickers and says, "Tough day on the water?"

Everyone roared in laughter, but I just walked to the tent and got a new set of warm clothes. That night as we were all falling asleep in the tent, Jamie said, "Thanks, Jeff." I told him don't worry about it. I lay in my sleeping bag and thought about the dynamic of having a brother. I didn't have one. But at that moment I realized what Todd felt often in having someone look up to him and have someone to look out for besides himself. It felt nice.

The third day was much like the second, but it started raining that evening. We listened to the rain as we fell asleep, and the cold wet air just soaked into everything. It was hard to sleep and get comfortable but late into the evening we just gave in to the exhaustion.

On the fourth morning it was extremely cold in the tent. When I zipped the door open, everything was white. It was the first part of June and there was an inch of snow on the ground. The guides said if we just waited an extra hour or two before heading out, the snow would melt as the air temp was rising quickly. So we had breakfast and sat around the fire as we watched the snow turn to slush and then melt completely in only about an hour. It was still misting out and the air was still. We headed out in the boat around 9 am.

5

"THE INCIDENT"

As we headed north past the islands we had fished before, we decided to go further. We were getting comfortable with the lake and felt like we had figured out how to easily navigate the areas we had been to so far. We looked at the laminated map in the boat at the islands and depths on the contour map and saw a channel we wanted to try to find. After an hour of traveling north, we located a large island called "Patton Island" which had a main shoreline on one side and a smaller island a short distance to its northwest. We wanted to fish the area between these two islands as they created a hump with deeper water on each side. It was a classic walleye area as they would chase baitfish into the shallow hump from both deep sides. There was no wind, and the water was smooth as glass. It was still very overcast as the light rain had just ended and a calm mist made the air feel cold and thick.

I had taken my rain gear off and was now wearing sweatpants, a hooded sweatshirt with a t-shirt layered underneath, and high-top leather Converse shoes. As we started trolling crankbaits back and forth over the hump, we watched a black bear swimming from the main shore to Patton Island. When it arrived at the beach, it paced back and forth as it shook itself dry. We watched it for about ten minutes as we fished. We had caught three small Northern Pike and had yet to catch a Walleye. The bear eventually entered the tree line of the island and disappeared. Both islands appeared to have a gravel beach that wrapped around the waterline. The beach appeared to be about 20 to 30 feet wide before it met the tree line. Each island stood above the water about 30 feet in elevation and was densely covered with tall pines, poplars, and birch.

Jamie reeled in his fishing rod and told Todd he had to take a piss. I knew what this meant, we were heading to shore. We had gone through this routine several times during the first few days of fishing as Jamie had a hard time peeing from a boat. He seemed to get upset when Todd teased him about it once, so I was fine with going to shore as it was a chance to stretch our legs and even explore a bit. I usually took advantage of these breaks to try to find a moose shed or something else that would be cool to take home. We headed to the southern beach of the smaller island next to Patton Island. As we neared the shoreline, we were careful to look into the water and make sure there were no jagged rocks or other structures other than the fine gravel bottom.

Once we pulled the motor up and touched the shore, I jumped out and pulled the nose of the boat up onto the beach a foot or two. We all walked along the beach and Todd commented on how still it was. You could hear the birds and ambient sound of the water's edge so clearly. As Todd would talk to us, his voice carried as we walked away from each other. The sound just flowed as if it reverberated in the cold humid air. Jamie stepped from the beach to the tree line and took his piss. I noticed a pathway at the edge of the beach. I walked over and stood at the edge of it as I looked closely at the gravel on the beach trying to figure out which animals were using it. It was wide at almost three feet, and it rose in elevation quickly as it went further from the beach. I couldn't see more than 20 feet up the trail as it had branched from large trees on each side of the path. It was firm and covered with pine needles, but it was very greasy from the rain and snow over the past 12 hours. I took two or three steps and my right foot just peeled back a step on the slippery surface.

Todd shouted over to me and asked what I was looking at and I told him it was a game trail. We questioned each other as to what animal would make such heavy use of the trail on this small of an island. I told Todd I was going to try to go up the trail and check it out. He was walking further down the beach exploring the opposite direction. I kept making my way up the trail, two steps up one step back. It was difficult to stay sure-footed and the elevation rose so quickly. I estimated it to be about a 25-to-30-degree incline in which the surface had no grip. I kept on moving up the trail and could tell

I was far above the beach and about 40 yards away from where I had entered the trail.

While struggling to gain my footing and holding onto a cedar scrub growing at the trail's edge, I heard a very loud crack. It sounded like lightning cracking in the wet air and it was very close. It came from the left side of the trail and was only about ten yards from my location. I stood like a statue as I looked at the trees and deadfall off the trail in that direction. I had been in this situation a few times before while hunting in both Northern Minnesota and Montana. I felt the sound was likely made by a Black Bear breaking a log or limb on the forest floor. The last thing I wanted to do was react in a panic and retreat in a way that would induce a pursuit. If it was a Black Bear with cubs, I could be in a dangerous situation, but it seemed unlikely a Sow would have its cubs on such a small island. It seemed more reasonable that it would be a single bear and if I would stand still and kept watching the area of the cracking sound, I would see movement. I stood and watched, waiting to see the black contrast among the collage of green, and brown and the black of the shadows.

Todd yelled up from the beach, "What was that?!"

I didn't answer him as I didn't want to make any sound as I stood there watching the trees. Todd yelled again, "Jeff! What's going on? Are you OK?" I could hear Jamie also calling out wondering what is going on.

I had stood there for almost two full minutes and still didn't see any movement. I was starting to wonder if perhaps a wet dead branch had broken off a tree or some other explanation. It didn't seem likely since there was no sound of anything falling or any follow-up noise of the original cracking snap. I looked down the trail and couldn't see the beach from all the overgrowth of branches in the canopy covering the trail. It was like looking through a narrow tunnel when you looked up or down the trail. It didn't sound like Todd or Jamie were coming up the trail, so I turned around to look back up the trail before starting my decline back down to the beach. As I turned my head, I was startled to find myself looking at the legs of something large only 10 feet away from my face.

They were two thighs right at eye level. It stood on an elevation about two feet higher than the ground I was standing on because of the upward incline. The thighs I was looking at were the diameter of two five-gallon buckets and were covered in dark hair. I looked upward as my eyes traveled up the body and realized it was standing on two legs, holding a five-foot section of birch log about 6 inches in diameter. The log had a small shallow root ball at one end and was broken at the other. I could see large fingers cradling it and wrapping around the underside of the log and curling up the surface. They looked like large human hands with hair all over the back of them, even on the backs of the fingers. It held this log at its waist with its arms outstretched downward. I looked above the log at its chest and noticed it was massively wide. There was no hourglass shape to this thing and as I looked upward at its shoulders and face it was apparent this was no animal familiar to me.

My mind was going through a checklist of all the things I was sure that I WASN'T looking at. It was not a brown bear, black bear, moose, or any other big game animal. It didn't appear to be a person as its massive size was simply too large. I leaned back as I looked up at its face, and it was like standing under a basketball hoop and looking straight up at the rim. Taking into consideration that it was standing about two feet above my ground height, its head stood almost five to six feet taller than mine. I was 6' and with the ground being about two feet higher where it stood than me, this thing was about 10' tall. Its face was human-like with a few exceptions. A strong pronounced brow line and the skin around its nose, mouth and eyes looked like dry cracked dirt. There was no sheen. It looked flat black in color where I could see the skin around its facial features and on areas of its hands. I only looked at its face for a moment and as soon as I saw its eyes it was like a bomb blast went off.

The birch log in its hands at its waist level was shucked towards me with a downward force that took me off my feet. It hit me in the waist and stomach, and I was in midair falling backward through the air. I could see its face react to me as I flew backward as it held its mouth with its lower lip curled down and out. Its eyes had a serious intent to their stare. It didn't look menacing or threatening, just serious and fixated on me. I hit the ground with a hard impact and the log landed on my chest and stomach. I slid quickly on my back and headfirst towards the beach. I looked back up the trail at it as I slid back and could see it stomp on the ground twice with such force, I could feel the impact through the firm wet ground in my back. I tried frantically to roll to my stomach as I slid backward. I wanted badly to get my feet underneath me to stop this downward backward slide. At this point, I wanted to be running rather than sliding out of control. I wrapped my leg around the log as it shifted lengthwise to my body as I slid. My right ankle became pinned underneath it and was sprained badly in the slide. I came to a stop at the edge of the beach and saw Todd running towards me. He was panicked as he was asking, "What's going on?!? Are you OK?"

As soon as I came to a stop from the slide, I got to my feet and was screaming at Todd and Jamie, "Get in the boat! Now! Get in the Boat!"

Jamie took off running towards the boat and he was the first one in. He got to the back and was lowering the motor. Todd ran to the boat and was pushing it back from the shore.

Todd kept yelling back to me, "Jeff, What's wrong! What was it?! What happened?" I couldn't take my eyes off the tree line. It felt like this thing was right behind me and I still couldn't explain what it was that attacked me.

I was shouting at Jamie, "Get the fucking motor started Jamie!"

Jamie was panicking and was struggling with the motor. Paul had pushed the boat a few feet off of the beach and Jam ie had the motor down but despite pulling the starter rope several times, it wasn't starting. I was side-stepping towards the boat across the beach, afraid to take my eyes off of the tree line. I couldn't run as my ankle couldn't bear any weight and I was limping as I tried to get to the boat. As I passed Todd at the front of the boat, he grabbed my sweatshirt and pulled me towards him, and yelled in my face asking me again, "What's going on?"

I kept staring at the tree line as I screamed back at him, "Get in the boat, we have to get out of here... get in the fucking boat!"

I grabbed the starboard edge of the gunwale and threw myself over the edge into the boat. Todd lifted himself over the nose of the boat and helped me get into the middle seat as I had landed on the floor of the boat and couldn't get my feet under me to get up. Jamie was still struggling to get the motor started. Todd went to the back of the boat and yelled for Jamie to get in the front. As Jamie crossed the middle seat, I saw his face. He was crying and was beside himself with fear. He sat down and I could hear Todd trying to start the motor.

Todd had been operating the motor all week and in retrospect, I'm not sure if Jamie had ever started a boat motor before. Maybe he didn't pump up the bulb to build fuel pressure, or maybe he had choked it and it was flooded. I just kept staring at that tree line. My mind was racing still trying to analyze and make sense of what was standing right in front of me. I've never seen anything like it before. Ten feet tall with a body that had to exceed a thousand pounds. I had seen adult record-size grizzly bears after they had been harvested by my fathers' clients and friends. They often weighed between 1100 and 1200 lbs. and were between 9 to 10 feet tall. This thing had a similar body mass and similar height but appeared more human.

At that point, Jamie started to freak out even more. There was a black bear on the beach about 100 yards down the shore from us and we were only about ten feet from the shoreline as we weren't drifting out. There was no breeze, and we were literally dead in the water. This black bear was walking towards us down the beach as it watched the tree line. It didn't take its eyes off the tree line as it just kept moving toward us as if it wasn't even aware we were there. Finally, it looked up at us and it switched from a slumbering walk to a quick gallop. It's as if it was excited to see us and that freaked out Jamie even more. As it closed the distance, I told Jamie to calm down and get the stringer that was hanging over the edge of the boat next to him. The stringer had the three-pike we had caught on it earlier. I told Jamie to take one of the fish and throw it up on the shore. I kept watching the tree line where the game trail was wondering if this thing was still there. Maybe that's what scared this bear to run onto the beach? Jamie threw the fish onto the shore towards the bear. This bear was not full-grown and was only about 250 lbs. As it stopped at the fish, it picked up the fish and stood on its back legs as it sat on its haunches. At that time, I noticed the bear was missing its left front paw. It held the Pike between its stub and in the other paw as it bit the head off the fish in one bite. Todd was still pulling the motor and was watching this all unfold. Jamie is still crying and panicked but I was trying to talk him through what to do next. I told him to grab the oar that was laying lengthwise down the edge of the seat and he pushed us out a bit and threw the oar back on the seats. The bear was facing us holding the fish but snapped its head towards the game trail and dropped the fish and took off running back down the beach in the direction it had come from. It was running full blast and Jamie was yelling at Todd and me about how the bear is running away.

The motor roared to life as Todd finally got it started. The bear was still running down the beach as I told Todd to keep backing up and get us off this island. Jamie kept asking me if the bear was what made the crashing sound on the trail I was on. I told him it wasn't what made the sound, and this made him start to go into panic mode all over again. Todd was slowly backing us up from the island in reverse. I was watching the beach and from about 70 yards away from the game trail, I watched that thing walk out onto the gravel. Todd and Jamie, both saw it and Jamie just started screaming.

Todd shouted, "What is that!? Jeff, what is that?" He repeated it over and over. Each time he asked, Jamie just reacted with more fear and panic. I felt like everything was moving in slow motion and the sound of their voices freaking out was just garbled. I was so focused on looking at this massive upright creature walking out onto the beach. It walked over to where the headless fish lay at the water's edge. With one fluid movement, it lowered itself with its shoulders at a 45-degree angle, grabbed the fish in its right hand and stood back up. It held it out in front of him as it looked at us. It stood there watching for almost 15 seconds. It then lowered the fish to its side and swiftly walked back into the tree line.

As soon as I lost sight of it, it felt as if someone unmuted the world and Jamie was screaming at me asking what that was. Todd was looking at me in shock as he tried to make sense of what he had just seen. I grabbed Jamie's leg and told him to stop screaming, we were ok now. We were safe. He was hyperventilating and crying, in total panic mode. He tried hard to catch his breath. The sounds he was making were like nails on a chalkboard making this whole ordeal so chaotic. My mind was struggling to make sense of it. Was it a human? How did it get that big? I could explain any of it in my head. Todd put the motor in gear, and we went full throttle in the direction of camp.

6

WHAT JUST HAPPENED?

After about five minutes, Todd slowed the boat and shut it off in the middle of the lake. Jamie had started to come down from his panic, but he was still crying. Todd asked me what happened on the trail and was that thing on the beach what knocked me down the trail? I spent about ten minutes telling Todd and Jamie everything that happened on the trail. We took turns asking each other questions that none of us could answer. What was it? Todd was the first one to use the term "Bigfoot".

He asked, "Could it have been a Bigfoot?"

Neither Todd nor I had grown up hearing much about Bigfoot. Despite being the sons of hunting guides and spending so much time in the wilderness big game hunting in Montana, Wyoming, Idaho, Minnesota, Michigan, Canada and even Alaska, we had never had a friend or relative tell us they had seen a Bigfoot. There were no stories shared around a campfire about Uncle Bob and his Bigfoot encounter. We had seen the PG film as kids during the Saturday matinee movie trailers at the cinema. But we literally grew up with no threshold of reference for Bigfoot.

"What else could it have been?" asked Todd.

I thought about that for quite a while and couldn't come up with a reasonable explanation. This was too remote to be a hoax. There wasn't anyone else out here. There were no cabins, no boats, and no people other than us and our fishing party. It had been four days and we saw no evidence of any humans. This was true off the grid, middle of nowhere, wilderness. The three of us concluded that we had just seen a Sasquatch. Telling myself that it was the only plausible explanation that fit was both surreal and uncomfortable. Todd was as uncomfortable with it as I was.

Knowing that's what it was and knowing how hard it is for us to process what just happened only made it more clear how it would be difficult for anyone else to process it without experiencing it. I felt we needed to get back to camp to tell his dad what had happened. Todd sat there quietly as he worked this out in his head, and he started to shake his head. "We can't," he said.

Jamie and I both told him that we had to. Someone needs to know what happened to us.

"They won't believe us. In their eyes, were the kids. We must be here for five more days with all of them, and they will do nothing but make fun of us. They will turn it into a joke. No one will believe us. No one. Jeff, this is MY dad, and I'm the one who must live with this decision, and I don't want to tell him or any of them. If you want to tell your dad when you get home, go ahead. But he won't believe you either. Unless you were here and seen this, how could anyone believe it?"

I didn't want to admit it, but maybe Todd was right. I agreed we wouldn't tell his dad. And we headed back to camp.

7

A GUIDES ADVICE

The ride back across the lake to the camp was difficult. We navigated it easily, but all three of us were in shock and each of us was handling it differently. Todd was simply focusing on the boat, the navigation, and finding a way to occupy his mind without being stuck on that beach, but undoubtedly, he was struggling. His demeanor didn't show his emotions often, but it had today. I had never seen him panicked before. I'm not sure if I had even heard him swear, but his filter had glitched during what happened. He remained emotionally intact enough to overcome the motor issue and stay composed enough to get us out of there. But regardless of how composed and how focused a person can be in the face of danger or of the unknown, Todd realized there was a place far beyond that and he had just found it.

As I found myself tormented by the inability to find reason with what we had experienced, I watched him on our way back, and I knew he was just as lost as I was searching for an explanation. Jamie was no longer panicked or in physical duress, but he was sobbing. Not audibly crying or wailing, but he couldn't stop the tears from flowing down his face in the wind of the boat ride. That look of fear had turned intoo a look of sadness. I understood Todd's reasoning for not wanting to tell his dad and the others. But this decision was going to mean that Jamie would have to find a way to deal with this on his own. The more I looked at his face, the more it made me sad too.

My ankle wasn't swollen, in fact, I hardly felt any pain at all. This seemed odd considering I couldn't bear any weight on it at all on the beach. I had taken my shoe off on the boat ride. My stomach and my left hip hurt. It felt scraped and bruised. It was getting warm out and I removed my sweatshirt and wore a grey t-shirt with the sweatpants. As we approached the dock, I put my shoe back on. Jamie kept looking at me as he wiped the tears from his eyes and I put my hand on his arm and told him, "It's going to be OK Jamie. Don't say anything and we can talk about it later tonight when they aren't around." Jamie nodded and tried to prepare himself for the greeting from the others on the dock. They were all there as they usually were for the mid-day routine of showing off the morning catch and having lunch. We tied off the boat and all three of us got out.

There was no celebration or bragging for us which I'm sure was confusing to the others. Todd's dad asked him if everything was alright, and Todd smiled and said "everything's fine." Everyone walked off the dock towards the firepit and lawn chairs. I stood on the dock and just stared back to the north toward the island. You couldn't see it from there, it was hidden behind several others, but I still found myself lost in my mind, on that trail. I was caught off guard by the oldest of the three guides who was walking down the dock.

"Is everything OK?" he asked.

I stared down at the water and didn't look him in the eyes as I answered, "Yes."

He was the oldest of the three brothers and was in his 60s. He was quiet and hadn't said much to me during our stay the previous 4 days.

He asked, "Did you get into an argument with your friends? Did something happen out in the boat?"

I told him, "Everything's fine, we're all fine."

He smiled and said, "Well something happened. If you don't want to tell them that's fine, but if you want to tell me, I won't say shit."

I looked at him and he was straight-faced and serious. "C'mon, let's take a walk," he said. I followed him off the dock and we walked down the wooded shoreline away from the others.

He told me his name was Daniel. I remembered that from when he introduced himself on day one, but maybe he thought I didn't remember. I told him my name is Jeff. He asked me what happened out there. I stood quietly looking at the lake contemplating whether I should tell him. I mean, if Todd didn't want to tell his dad and his family, I'm fine with that. But I needed to talk to somebody. Maybe it was my hope that this guy spent his entire life here at this lake. Or maybe it was his Inuit heritage and I felt maybe he would give me a chance to tell him what happened before he started laughing at me. Either way, I told him that something had happened out there on a small island we had stopped on. He was immediately intrigued. I must have taken 15 minutes telling him every detail of what happened. He had asked where this had happened, and I told him on Patton Island. I knew it wasn't on Patton Island but on the small Island next to it, but the small island didn't have a name on the map and if I told him Patton Island, he would at least know the area we were.

He said, "Let me show you something."

Daniel led me down a small path to an old run-down wooden boat house they had made out of quarter-sawn lumber decades ago. It was run down and weathered, and the door was falling off of it. It looked like they still used it to store boat gas, motor parts, and other utility items. On the back side of it was an aluminum Lund guide series boat flipped upside down on the ground with a tarp stretched over it held down by large rocks. He pulled the tarp off it and the entire starboard side from the front V to the stern was caved in. It looked as if had been sitting on a road and someone had hit it with a motorcycle. The caved-in part had a prominent V where it had been struck. I asked him what happened? He proceeded to tell me the following account.

The three brothers spent most of their time in any given year guiding moose and bear hunts. During the previous fall, 8 months ago, Daniel was guiding a moose hunter in the northern area of the lake. They had spotted a decent bull on one of the islands and they decided to beach their boat well down the shore from the moose. The hunter ended up harvesting the bull and they went and took pictures of the hunter with the moose. Then Daniel brought the hunter back to camp as they were losing light and Daniel returned to the island himself to skin and quarter out the moose. He felt it would be pretty easy since the bull hell on the gravel beach of the island and it wouldn't require much footwork to pack out the moose as most of their hunts did. He had skinned it and quartered the bull and had carried the front left quarter to the boat. It was heavy but he had gotten it loaded without issue.

As he was walking the short distance back to the moose, something large screamed at him and charged him from the tree line. He said he ran to the boat and jumped inside of it trying to place something between him and what was charging him. He said this creature stood over nine feet tall and weighed over 1,000 lbs. and was so massive. It stood like a human. It ran like a human but with more speed and power. It ran up to the edge of the boat and started throwing its knee into the side of it. Over and over, it struck the boat while it screamed and just caved in the side. Seven or eight strikes and the boat had caved in on that side. He had gotten out of the boat on the opposite side and tried to reach his rifle, but it was on the floor of the boat, and he couldn't get to it without getting closer to this thing. After caving in the side of the boat, it screamed at him as it grabbed the front quarter by the leg and with one hand lifted it up and threw it over its shoulder, and ran into the tree line. Daniel got into the boat and grabbed his rifle but couldn't tell where it was, it had disappeared in the shadows of the tree line.

Daniel grabbed the handheld radio and called his brothers and told them he had an emergency and needed them right away. They were en route from the opposite end of the lake as they were scouting hunting areas on the far south side. Daniel said he sat there by the boat with his rifle waiting for almost 20 minutes while this thing kept screaming at him. It was angry and he could hear it pacing through the trees but never could see it. As he heard his brothers approaching in their boat from a mile away, this thing seemed to leave.

Daniel sat there and pondered how he would explain what happened to his brothers and whether they would believe him. He decided that he would tell him that he was charged by a cow moose, and it rammed the boat because he felt there was no way they would believe what happened. After living there their entire lives, none of them had experienced anything to do with Bigfoot. They grew up hearing tales from their relatives but none of them were certain if it was real. When they first arrived, they could tell

Daniel was scared out of his mind. They asked him what happened, and he tried to tell them about the cow moose charging him and ramming the boat. As they loaded the quartered moose into his brother's boat, Daniel stood watching the tree line. One of them asked about the missing quarter and Daniel told them the truth about what happened.

As I stood there listening to Daniel share this story with me, I found myself feeling a strange sense of relief. It felt like Todd, Jamie, and I had been stranded on a deserted island, and there was someone else who was there. I know that sounds like a weird analogy, but it was such a relief to hear an adult convey the news that we weren't losing our minds by simply sharing a story that, in the end, said I believe you. I asked him if his brothers believed him when he told them. He said that despite the boat right there with the caved inside, one brother believed him and one didn't. He said he is wrestling with that. His little brother doesn't believe this happened despite the evidence.

Daniel went on to give me the following advice. "Nothing good is going to come from telling others about what happened to you. Unless they were there, or in a similar situation, they simply aren't capable of being able to process the idea that this is real. That's on them, not on you. But nothing good will come of telling others. You best find a way to get your mind back to where it was your first four days here and just try to enjoy the remainder of your stay. It's not easy, and it's only been 8 months since this happened to me, but I don't see how my situation with my brother will change unless he has an experience. And if I could take back the decision to tell him, I would. Feeling like someone so close to you doesn't believe you is probably the most painful thing I've ever felt in this life."

He went on to ask if I was injured. I said I twisted my ankle, but it was ok. He then pointed to the bottom of my shirt by my left hip, and it was soaked with blood. He lifted it up and I had a scrape down my left hip the size of my hand from the log. I lifted my shirt up and my entire stomach was already black and blue. He said he would put some bandages in my tent while everyone else was eating and I should change my shirt.

8

A DAMAGED INNOCENCE

That night in our tent, after we left the campfire and Todd, Jamie, and I retired for the evening, we had a chance to discuss again what had happened. Jamie just laid there on his sleeping bag looking and listening to Todd and me. I shared with them both what had happened to me on the trail. We talked about what we had all seen on the beach. We shared our thoughts comparing opinions on its size and weight. What we noticed about its appearance. The length of the hair as it flowed off its arms. The way it walked so fluidly. None of us heard it make any vocalization whatsoever. After about an hour, Todd said, "I'm done. I don't want to talk about it anymore."

Jamie asked him, "You mean anymore tonight? Or anymore ever?"

Todd rolled over and said, "Ever."

That night it started raining again. I couldn't sleep as I lay there for hours in my sleeping bag. My mind was racing, and it wouldn't quit." I knew Todd was asleep, but I wasn't sure about Jamie. I heard him roll over, so I looked in his direction.

He was looking at me and said, "Thanks, Jeff."

"For what Jamie?" I asked.

Tears were running down his face and he said, "For helping me. I don't understand why this had to happen to us." I told him to try to think about something else and get some sleep.

I lay there still fixated on the same questions and failing to find answers that made sense. I listened to Jamie for the next few hours trying not to make any sound while he cried. I started thinking about Todd and me and how we are starting new chapters in our lives. I'm going into the Army in just a few weeks. A few years of adventure and new people, new friends, and new places. Todd was going off to school out of state. New friends, new adventures. But Jamie, he was going to be a freshman in high school. Todd and I were popular in school. We had large friend groups, played sports and we didn't have a problem fitting into any circle. That wasn't the case for Jamie. I didn't know him well, but I had heard talk about how Jamie didn't fit in well. He struggled with making friends and dealt with depression and self-esteem issues. Jamie was going to be dealing with the repercussions of what happened today on his own. There's no one he can talk to about it. And Todd deciding not to tell anyone made it difficult for Jamie not to follow suit. It didn't seem fair for Todd to make that decision without taking into consideration as to how it would affect his little brother.

When I think back on that day, 35 years later, I realize how much difference there was between Jamie and Todd and I. I am now a father of two sons, 17 and 18 years old. They are capable outdoorsmen and have done well learning about the wilderness and their surroundings. But one thing that is very clear to me is the difference in how they process things now at their age and how they did when they were 13 and 14 years old. It's a night and day difference. How they handle adversity and challenges now makes me feel as if I can turn off my "worry" switch. That was not the case four years ago. Their maturity and confidence levels simply weren't advanced. When I think about how Jamie was coming undone during all that chaos, I realize how damaged he may have become if he didn't have help dealing with it after the fact. I never really talked to Jamie much once I left for the military. Todd and I spoke when we saw each other at Christmas or when our paths crossed over the coming years, but we didn't remain that close. I see him every year or two and the last time we spoke, I asked him if he ever thinks about that day in Manitoba at Granville Lake. He said, "Jeff, I've spent every day since then trying to forget about what happened that day." I asked him if he ever told his dad before he passed away, and he said he didn't. He said Jamie is married and has a couple kids and is doing fine but he doesn't talk about it either. I asked Todd if Jamie still likes to fish. He said, Jamie doesn't hunt, doesn't fish, doesn't camp...he lives in the city and isn't comfortable in the outdoors. At that moment, I realized that Todd had made the wrong decision.

On my drive home from seeing Todd, I decided to pull down an old logging road that led back to an area where I had a tree stand on the edge of Big Mantrap Lake. I sat on the hood of my truck looking out at the water and listened to the blue jays and redwing blackbirds raise their ruckus over my presence. I spent the better part of the afternoon thinking about all the things God had blessed me with in this life. My family, my opportunities I spend in the outdoors, my home, my career, friends, were all things that came to mind. There was a lot and I was not blind to the fact that I had reason to feel grateful and find joy in all of it. But it made me realize something that made me feel sad when thinking about Jamie. You could rob me of my money, I'd find a way to make more. You could steal my car, and I'd buy another. You could burn down my house, and the insurance would pay to rebuild it. If my friends abandoned me, Eventually I would replace them too. But there were two things I could not replace if you took them away from me. My family was one of them. The other was my passion to want to be in the outdoors. My ability to be comfortable regardless of how remote I found myself. If someone figured out a way to rob you of that, how do you get it back?

9

A REASON FOR SILENCE

On July 23, 1987, I left for Ft. Knox for basic training in the US Army. The 8 weeks I spent there were extreme, to say the least. I thought I was in shape, but I guess "in shape" is simply a matter of perspective. In shape for what?

My platoon was made up of 30 young men who represented every section of America geographically and racially. Each person had joined the military for different reasons. I was there because I was a good athlete, but not good enough to obtain a full ride. I was smart but not smart enough for an academic scholarship. My family was middle class and there was no college fund set up or second mortgages to be had to send me to college. If I wanted to go, I had to figure out how to pay the bill and the Army was the answer.

That wasn't the case for others in my platoon. Many were there out of a sense of pride. Their father had served and their father's father and now it was their turn. Others were there because they had gotten in trouble with the law and a judge told them they had two choices. Either go to jail or go into the military. There were one or two who had been dumped by a girlfriend and in their despair, they joined the military. My advice would be to not do that. It's an extreme answer to a simple problem that likely could have been fixed by asking her best friend out on a date.

Basic training is designed to build a team of people who recognize a need for each other to survive. This was a new concept for me because most of my outdoor skill set was designed to save yourself. Your Drill Sergeants did not care if you were popular in high school. They didn't care if you were ugly or attractive, short, or tall, or anything else you may have thought made you special. These 30 strangers replaced everything you left behind. They were now your best friend, your parents, your siblings, and your neighbors. They were now your everything because they were all that was there. We were broken down as a group. We were disassembled of anything that made us an individual and we were put back together with an understanding that I needed the person next to me as much as they needed me. And because of that mentality, we became very effective at everything we did. You learned to communicate with and respect each other because we were no longer jocks, geeks, burnouts, or any other clique we used to use to identify ourselves.

After Basic Training, I went to Redstone Arsenal in Huntsville, AL. I was there for AIT (Advanced Individual Training) to attend munitions school and Explosive Ordinance School. Redstone Arsenal is the most spied-upon base in the military. I was issued a security clearance there and the process to obtain it required an extensive background check and personality analysis. In short, the Army wanted to be assured they weren't giving access to these secured areas to some kid who had psychological issues or social glitches that would make them easy targets to be compromised by foreign intelligence agencies. It seemed over the top but when you considered what they did at Redstone, it was necessary protocol.

Redstone had an underground facility that was comparable in shape and size to a small city. There were several levels underground that were utilized to develop and test warfare technology. Weapons systems, defense systems, etc. They asked me all kinds of odd questions about my past, my upbringing, my moral character, and my mental stability and by the end of the process, I realized there was no way they would give this clearance to me had I ever told them or anyone in my unit that I had been attacked by a Sasquatch a few months ago. I'm pretty sure that would have been grounds for them to question my mental stability. I held that clearance for several years as I served with the 29th Infantry and other various EOD teams. My military service would offer no opportunity to find anyone I would ever feel comfortable talking to about what happened that day at Granville Lake in Manitoba.

After I completed my enlistment, I left the military with a resume that included operating a firing range on the Malone Complex in Ft Benning, GA, working at the Airborne School in Ft Benning, and serving in Desert Storm on an EOD team inside of the "Kill Box". I was ready to get out and do something different. I attended Columbus College and got a degree in Business. I never felt close enough to anyone in college to develop the kind of trust it would take to open up and share my encounter. After college, I worked in Sales Management and met a girl who I eventually married. After six years of marriage, we had two sons. I went on to obtain a real estate license and after two years in real estate, I got my Broker's license. I started a real estate firm in Sioux Falls, SD and opened a second one in Northern Minnesota.

During these years of building my business, I continued to enjoy the outdoors. I guided Mule Deer and Pheasant hunters on my family's land in South Dakota. I guided elk and deer hunters on land I had contracted in Wyoming and Montana. And I took annual trips hunting in Idaho, Alaska, Manitoba, and

Saskatchewan. When I wasn't hunting, I spent weekends taking my kids fishing, camping, and kayaking and we explored something new every chance we got.

Despite all of that, I hadn't told my wife that I had an encounter with a Sasquatch. The risk versus the reward just didn't ass up. She was a farm girl from Iowa. She didn't have a lot of experience in the outdoors other than working on their farm. What if she had doubts about my sincerity or integrity? If she had no exposure to the possibility of the existence of Sasquatch, how is she going to be able to comprehend that her husband stood in front of one and had a log thrown at him? I simply didn't see the value in risking our trust in each other over something that I had gotten used to not talking about by this point.

As my real estate business grew, I started working with developers and investors on many projects. They turned out to be very lucrative for me and my relationships with them grew stronger. There were three of them that I considered more than business partners. We did a lot together aside from business as we would go on vacations, hunting trips, and other adventures. Their families became close to my family. There were many times I wanted to open up and share my encounter with them. They had become my best friends. But they trusted me with millions of dollars of investment capital. The risk of sharing this encounter with anyone just kept growing bigger and bigger the older I got. I simply couldn't afford to have them question my integrity.

10

KILLING THE RISK

There was no doubt that not ever talking to anyone about my encounter had posed a burden on me over the years. I felt the weight of it. It was a secret that I found to be both heavy and annoying.

After 18 years of marriage, my wife and I got divorced. We remained close and still did things as a family. In fact, we still shared a lake home and found ourselves still being best friends as we shared our responsibilities as parents and did our best to maintain our shared social circles and friends.

One night I walked out into the living room of our lake house and found her sitting on the couch listening to a podcast. I asked her what she was listening to, and she said a show on Bigfoot. "This guy is sharing this story about how he saw Bigfoot and it's so freaking crazy! Jeff, this guy saw one!" I stood there in the middle of the room watching her facial expressions of intrigue and amazement as she listened to this podcast.

I walked out onto our deck and sat there looking out at Lake Belle Taine. After she was done listening to the podcast, she walked out onto the deck with two beers and sat one in front of me. She asked, "Are you ok? What's wrong?" I sat there both nervous and apprehensive but decided that this was it. I was going to tell the person that mattered most to me and the one I had assessed to be the highest risk with the most to lose about my encounter. I asked her if she thought the guy on the podcast had seen Bigfoot? She said, "Yes! Why? You don't believe they exist? It's ok if you don't, but I do. Why couldn't they? There 'are way too many reports of people seeing them for them to not be real." I tipped that bottle of beer back and emptied it and sat there and smiled at the irony that was playing out here. I told her, "I'm about to share something with you that happened over 30 years ago. When I was 18." Her eyes lit up and she sat back and listened to me tell her about my encounter in Manitoba for over an hour. I shared every detail. I told her how it had affected me. I cried as I shared how badly Jamie had come undone during the encounter. I told her how I was afraid to tell anyone throughout my time in the military and in college. I shared with her how I felt like I would have lost my friends and business partners had I told any of them. She replied, "Well I am glad you finally told me."

It's hard to explain the sense of being unburdened by this weight to someone who has never carried it. I had gotten tired of carrying it. I found that I had reached a point where I didn't care about the risk anymore. I had given the risk more credit than it deserved. The risk no longer felt like it carried the bite that I feared that it did. I no longer found it to be such a concern that someone may not believe me. I didn't feel that burden was mine to bear. I had come to recognize that everyone is on their own journey of discovery in this life. The threshold of proof each person requires to believe in anything was different for each person. Whether it was a belief in God, gravity, or Bigfoot, it didn't matter. Each person was on their own path of discovery and whether they reached their destination wasn't up to me, it was up to them. From that point on, if I shared my encounter with anyone, I did so in hopes that it helped them on their journey of discovery, but I no longer took the responsibility of getting them there. If you don't believe me, I'll still wake up tomorrow and go on living. This was true whether it was a stranger or a million-dollar business partner.

I started sharing my experience with fellow hunting guides that I had known for years. These people had found themselves in the same remote parts of nowhere as I had throughout their lives and to my surprise, many of them had their own experiences. Several shared times where they either found themselves in view of Bigfoot or having things happen that they couldn't explain. It seemed the more I shared the encounter, the more I found others who had been looking for an opportunity to share their own stories. I started to research local encounters through different online databases. I learned that there were several recent encounters in the areas of Northern Minnesota. Many of those areas were in the Pine Island Forest and Boundary Waters where I had spent years archery hunting and kayaking. As I learned more about those who had been looking to prove this creature's existence, I took note of the techniques they used to capture pictures or videos. It seemed to be a very low success ratio.

By nature, I would describe myself as a problem solver. I'm always looking for a more efficient method of accomplishing something. I tend to observe what makes something work as well as what would make it work better. I think this tendency is inherent, but I also feel my time in the military advanced it to a level that I admit could be considered obsessive. As I started to become familiar with the techniques and tactics being utilized by those researching the existence of Bigfoot, one thing stood out. There is very little factual evidence outside of the PG footage, a few castings that seem to authentically show dermal ridges, and a handful of audio recordings that seem to have an origin that isn't in a database of known sounds and ranges made by recognized animals. And yet, many researchers seemed to be speaking factually on the theories they have developed around Bigfoot. I found this troubling.

In order to advance the science behind this mystery, we need to be able to educate each other on the things we discover, share our ideas and theories, and be able to approach those ideas with the same tenacity to prove them unlikely as we do to prove them plausible. And somehow, we are supposed to do this without pissing each other off. That's a tall order. Most in this community are passionate about the things they believe to be true even if there is no factual evidence to prove they are true. This makes communication among some in the research community a challenge. Instead of focusing on the 90% we share when it comes to theory and investigation, we choose to poison each other with the 10% we disagree on. I have come to realize that this is one of the biggest obstacles we face in advancing the science and having those outside of the Bigfoot community take a fair look at the possibility that this is a very real creature.

11

THE PREDICTIVE HYPOTHESIS

When an experiment yields positive results (in support of the predictive hypothesis), a repetition that confirms the original results is called "replication. " Replication by independent investigators is one of the hallmarks of science." according to the Scientific Institute.

When applying this to Bigfoot research, one starts to wonder why more researchers aren't yielding positive results? I think the problem isn't in the effort, but rather in the expectation. To have a defined goal of expectation, you must first have a theory or predictive hypothesis you are testing. And that is where we tend to drop the ball. For example, if you plan to go out this weekend with a couple buddies to try to find evidence of bigfoot, you may do several things while out in the field. You may go about employing these tactics like tree knocking or imitating a vocalization to get a response. You may even be prepared to record such a response. You now are attempting to solicit a response to record it, but what is your predictive hypothesis?

Leon Thompson is a mental health professional and active in

the bigfoot community studying behavioral tendencies in people's encounters and experiences. Leon and I have had several conversations about how research into the Sasquatch mystery seems to be stuck. Why are so many not looking outside of the creative and psychological parameters that have been set in research techniques? And who is responsible for setting them?

Leon went on to tell me about a term called "perseveration". It is closely related and often employed parallel to Parkinson's Law of Triviality. It means "When a system is more interested in defending the idea of the topic than dealing with the evidence of the topic." In Florida, there was an air emergency involving two pilots in a plane. The plane experienced a warning light coming on saying the landing gear was not properly deployed. They flew by the tower to visually verify if it was just the light malfunctioning or if the gear was not down? The tower radio's back that they couldn't tell on the first pass. It appeared to be down but was it all the way down and locked in? They flew past a second time, then a third. Both the pilots and the tower crew were so preoccupied with trying to focus on solving this landing gear issue, they did not realize that the plane was about to run out of fuel, and on their last attempt they ran out of fuel and crashed. The lesson here is, don't be solely prefixed with the wrong problem with a want to achieve the wrong data. Tunnel vision and a closed mind often lead to missing crucial information.

Our brain fixates on a programming system that is a default system. It reverts to that when considering unfamiliar processes. When considering new processes, one tends to consider the unfamiliarity and the non-guarantee that it will be successful, and we are reluctant to revert away from the default process. This isn't an issue of reverting back to it; the issue is that we rarely revert away from it.

Leon went on to tell me about "repetition compulsion". As the term suggests, it's when we employ a tendency to stick with the "tried and true". But if it were true, it would likely be producing results. Sasquatch research seems to be providing more theories and opinions to debate than it is definitive results. One might be tempted to consider, what are we researching if we are only duplicating these failed, "in the box" type of tactics in advancing the science that produces no definitive results? Applying the scientific method isn't a guarantee for positive results. Many times, it fails. Adjustments to the way its applied need to be made to not duplicate another failure. If those adjustments aren't made and we just keep copycatting each other's same applications, why would we feel as if it would produce a different result? Don't get me wrong, I admit that these applications do yield experiences. A knock or vocalization may illicit one in return. Or the same type of camera set up in the same way as you hear others doing it may produce another blurry picture. But it is being done repetitiously a million times with little results. It may simply require another method or a slight modification to the process to yield something different.

One other thing that Leon mentioned to me is a term called "Illusionary truth effect."

If you hear something enough times, you process it as a fact. Until you can accept and develop the brain's ability to think outside of the box, you can't realistically consider a new process. It's commonly referred to as lazy thinking. The Illusionary Truth Effect is evident in every area of research as so many have had their thought process hijacked by the Kool-Aid drinking. They forget what something else tastes like or even that something may taste better. Let alone be more nutritious to the process. People have a trust regulator, and they subscribe to certain sources as being trustworthy. When they receive a new prospective process and it isn't from a cataloged trusting source, it has a lower receptive chance to be considered.

Sometimes we become laser-focused not on the fact that we are right, but on the fact that there is no way we can be wrong. If you are programmed to follow yourself at all costs, you are not capable to identify the cracks in your beliefs. There are no experts at this point, and that includes all of us. I have yet to find a university offering a Doctorate Degree in Sasquatch Research. We are all the students, and we are all the professors. We share our ideas and theories to not only inform others of our experiences but also to get feedback that may make us reconsider what we gleaned from them. A seemingly hard lesson to learn is that you don't have to like someone to be able to learn something from them. I find myself watching YouTube episodes and listening to podcasts from all kinds of personalities and if I'm being honest, some of them are hard to agree with at times. Does that mean I can't learn something from them? Absolutely not.

There are those in the Sasquatch community that spend way too much time fixating on the things they disagree with someone on rather than paying attention to the common ground they share. As mentioned before, I think that the tendency to try to poison each other over the 10% we don't agree on instead of trying to advance the science in the 90% we do is dangerous for the community. I do not believe that another human exists on this Earth that I could endorse 100% of their beliefs. That doesn't stop me from searching for the information that benefits us both if we can respectfully communicate.

Leon concluded that when scientists study primates, they never put or assume human traits on the species they are studying. Same with dogs or other pets. The dog perceives you as equal to another dog, not some profound intelligent being way above them in intellectual capability. They simply love the way you smell and that you feed and pet them. When you treat a dog like a human, it starts to not have a chance to be a dog anymore. They are meeting your expectations of human traits.

The "appearance of ourselves to others" is more important to many than simply being ourselves. That is why so many can't fess up to a flaw or mistake they made online or in public. Our own stubbornness and our resistance to admitting being wrong have gotten worse over time due to the accountability to thousands in the online audience instead of the few in real-life interaction. We need to get comfortable with the fact that we COULD be wrong in anything that we do. I won't point any fingers or mention any names, but a good clue is "porcupine" if you are looking for a good example of this.

12

A HIGH-VALUE TARGET

After spending decades guiding hunters in remote areas, I was enjoying the time I spent in northern Minnesota. The summers were fun on the lake, fishing, swimming, kayaking, and watching the kids enjoy lake life. The winters aren't for everybody. It gets very cold for about four months a year. All the lakes freeze over with several feet of ice. Everything turns white and it snows often. I love to ice fish and snowmobile. I take a snowmachine out often in remote areas. There's something about the solace and aloneness that amplifies when it's all covered in snow. Running a trail or up a snow-covered frozen river until you are in the middle of a forest and just shutting off the machine. That's a kind of quiet and alone that many never get to experience.

Two years ago, on a day in January, I found myself doing just that. In the middle of the Pine Island Forest after running up the Clearwater River and through the densely forested landscape I stopped in a clearing. The clearing seemed almost misplaced. It was about the size of a football field and surrounded by tall Pines, Poplars, and Birch trees. After traveling through the trees and zigzagging around all the deadfall trees, it was weird to ride into a void of all of that. I was intrigued enough to grab my phone and pull up google maps and look at the area in detail. I identified other seemingly open isolated areas like this one. I pinpointed six of them on the GPS map. I spent the afternoon traveling to all of them. They were within a four-mile range of each other. Little open clearings in the middle of dense forest.

The initial reason I marked these areas was that I am always looking for new areas to hang tree stands for archery hunting deer. I like to archery hunt over a deer decoy during pre-rut and rut and deer seem to be more susceptible to coming to a decoy when they can visually see it from a distance. The small open areas made for perfect stand locations. During the coming weeks, I had met a fellow hunting guide who I had known for years. He shared with me an experience he had in the Pine Island Forest near the Red Lake Reservation border. As he was telling me of this experience, I could see that he was visibly shaken while recounting it. This was a friend I had known to be very trustworthy and what I would describe as a straight shooter. He wasn't the type to seek attention or embellish things.

The story he shared with me for almost an hour wasn't just a story. You could tell by his face, his expressions, and his breathing that he was in duress not only while experiencing it but also in its retelling. The account involved a time when he had hung a tree stand about 3 miles into the forest after accessing the area from a UTV trail. It was northeast of an area called Debs, MN. Debs isn't even a town really, it's an intersection of the road where there were a few acreages in one area. He had placed the stand and hiked out to the UTV and the next day he returned with a handsaw to clear some overhanging branches that covered his shot lanes from the stand. As he was approaching the stands' location, he said he heard what he described as a woman's scream, and it was long and drawn out. It seemed almost too long in duration, over 20 seconds, to be done without stopping to take a breath. He looked up ahead at where the stand had been hung and it was destroyed. He said he didn't believe it to be someone trying to steal it and it didn't seem to be done by a "normal person".

I asked him what he meant by that, and he went on to explain how the 16' steel ladder was ripped from the stand's base and the rungs were worn apart from the side frame rails in four different spots and the entire length was bent in half. The stand itself had the standing platform ripped off it with the seat connected. All that was left on the tree were the side stand rails that were strapped to the tree with heavy tie-down straps. I asked if he thought a bear could do the damage? He agreed a bear would have the strength to do it but when you considered the intricacy involved with tearing the rungs apart in the way it was damaged it just seemed too systematic. This wasn't random destruction like it's torn from a base and bent, it was bent in half, folded in two with rungs torn from it. I agreed that it seemed odd for a bear to do that much intricate damage to a stand rather than just ear it down with its weight from climbing it. This damage seemed to be a message rather than random. He said he left the stand there and never went back.

I took that opportunity to share my encounter with him which happened to me in 1987 in Manitoba. When I was done telling him about it, he replied, "They're real." I asked him if he had heard from others in our area of local encounters or experiences that people had a hard time explaining. He said he had heard from others that there had been 3 recent accounts in that small area of Debs MN, all by separate individuals.

This intrigued me so I started asking other guides in the area about any experiences they may have had. I had found recorded accounts of encounters and talked to two separate individuals who had encounters from the Itasca Forest area North of Park Rapids, up to Bemidji, around Red Lake as well as Debs. I started to study the topography and the forestation of this triangular area that stretched about 50 miles by 30 miles. There were lakes both large and small in the area, lots of them. Waterways that connected the lakes intertwined through the entire area. And the six clearings I had mapped out that January day was right in the middle of them.

13

A DIFFERENT APPROACH

Towards the end of the winter, I had been thinking about how I could use these areas I had pinpointed in a way I could explore whether these encounter sites were being used for habituation by Sasquatch. There were simply too many encounters occurring in this area. Could there be an established population of them and if so, how many? My mind was flooded with questions. If I were to try to examine these areas what techniques and tactics would prove without question that they were there? Trail cams? I had already had over a dozen trail cams out in the forest and hadn't seen anything that would make you think it was a Sasquatch. Even the pictures of black bear revealed accurately what I was looking at.

Wood knocking? I had heard hundreds of accounts of people knocking and successfully receiving knocks back. But what did they conclusively prove? Could it have been people knocking back? Maybe. Maybe not. There was no conclusive proof. Besides, I wasn't convinced it was a good idea to try to communicate with something in a language I didn't know how to speak. The community is overrun with speculation that one knock means this, two means that, five means run like hell, etc. So many different opinions and none of them are based on any significantly replicated data.

Vocalizations, whooping, whistling, chatter, and screams? Again, a language I am not familiar with, and what they are communicating to each other. I had no problem identifying almost any sound made by area wildlife. coyotes, wolves, moose, Deer, bears, bobcats, lynx, and mountain lions, I had heard it all and had examined the range of sound each of those species could make. But I still didn't know what they were saying. I knew what they sounded like, but I didn't know what they were saying. If I didn't know how to speak Chinese but tried to draw a bunch of Chinese letters on a sheet of paper and showed it to a person who could interpret it, how do I know I didn't unknowingly write something to the effect of "Do you want to fight?" I may regret trying to communicate in a way I am not familiar with.

Audio recording devices? I was up in the air about audio recording because many of those who had used them and successfully captured sounds they couldn't attribute to a recognized or referenced source still had no way to prove what the source is. Although I feel that data is useful and interesting, it wasn't conclusive to prove these creatures were out there. The other thing I was uncomfortable with was the disagreement that exists as to what a Sasquatch is capable of sensing. Battery presence, IR Flashes, Motion Detection, UV Coatings on lenses, and hard plastic, everyone had their own opinions. And no one had any conclusive data showing that any or all of them were detectable.

A body? That would certainly be conclusive if you managed to produce a body. But I wasn't comfortable with the idea of trying to harvest one without knowing its origin or full capability. That was out of the question based on my own ethics and the uncertain accountability for such an action.

Looking for castable prints or forest language? Many are doing that. Many are finding interesting things in the forests with tree structures, tree bends, breaks, etc. I felt that although these could be evidence when combined with other data from the same location, on their own, it's not conclusive. The debates were rampant in the community on tree bends and structures. They ranged from what nature is capable of in snow load, wind, flooding, etc. Could a human replicate what you are looking at, sometimes yes, and sometimes no, but still inconclusive as to the existence of Sasquatch in any given area. Castable prints however are slightly more intriguing and with a growing database of prints that have been cast revealing dermal ridges and midtarsal breaks etc., they certainly helped us understand possible locomotion and possible development, but they simply weren't common. In our area, the forest floor was covered with a thatch of pine needles and rock. Many of the rivers had gravel composition with sand and although they would reveal a general shape if you discovered one, it likely wouldn't reveal dermal ridges. Plus, there are so many bears in our area, anyone who has looked at proposed Sasquatch track pictures knows how many double bear prints exist in what's being brought forth. Tracks were something I would keep looking for but I didn't feel it was a good tactic to simply just roam around through a few hundred thousand acres of the forest looking specifically for tracks that wouldn't likely reveal enough data to prove they were there.

What's left? So many tactics are being used with so few conclusive results. I decided to break this down and take a hundred steps back. Get out of the box. Stop only considering what everyone else was doing. Stop focusing on what was working because nothing was working to a conclusive level. Let's consider what isn't working, set it aside, and stop focusing on it. What is the objective here?

If I was going to step into a clearing in an area I suspected they could exist based on recent accounts, how could I establish a simple technique to determine if they were? In this process, you find yourself playing devil's advocate and trying to expose any proposed tactics vulnerability to fail at the objective. The interesting thing is that as you adjust each tactic to overcome the vulnerability, I found that it seemed to be a matter of simplifying it and not complicating it. When you step back from the puzzle and look at it from a distance, you find yourself not questioning the method, you find yourself analyzing the subject of study.

In this case, we can't solely develop our analysis of Sasquatch based on what science has shown us, but rather what could we safely conclude based on what we all seem to agree on. It's significantly larger than a normal human. It's covered in hair on most of its body. Their main objective in the element of survival is to remain elusive and avoid what they would perceive to be a threat, humans. They seem to be capable of employing a high level of reasoning in decision-making like many primates. They spend every waking moment in the elements and wilderness and because of that, they likely are far beyond any human ability to move throughout environments both quietly and relatively undetected. In this analysis of what they are likely capable of, I choose to detect anything from a supernatural perspective and only consider that which something flesh and blood are capable of. No portals, no mind speak, no teleporting, etc.

I'm not saying they couldn't be capable of something like that, it's just not what I felt I could conclude with any confidence since I've never seen a portal, a working model of a portal, etc. I'm simply sticking to what is plausible and most likely when considering all the options. Throughout this process I found myself asking the same question as a baseline of consideration. What is its biggest vulnerability? What could be considered the weakest link in its physical and mental composition? The answer I came up with was its own curiosity. If it is capable of thought processes like humans and other primates, it must be curious about things it doesn't understand. When it analyzes something to determine if it is a threat or not, it would have to navigate a subjective process and assess different attributes of any possible threat.... which means it is curious.

I can look back on my own life and attest that many of the most dangerous situations I have often faced were born from curiosity. Putting yourself in a position where your curiosity exposes you to vulnerability is to be human. If they were like us in so many ways, then leveraging their curiosity had to be the foundation of the techniques or tactics I would try to employ. Not relying on happenstance to create that perfect storm of opportunity of walking up on one, or catching a fleeting image on a camera, but rather creating a situation in which it perhaps hadn't been analyzed before. Something unfamiliar meant to create a level of curiosity that simply overrode its own discretions.

A few days after determining the direction I wanted to go, I was yet to determine how to get there. I was standing in a Walmart in the sporting goods section looking at a bin composed of bungee cords filled with rubber balls. $2.97 for a rubber ball that was about 15" round. I picked one up and squeezed it and noticed how flimsy it felt. The rubber wasn't very thick, and I set it on the ground and stepped on it. It compacted easily. Anything with claws could puncture this with minimal pressure. I bought two of them, a red one and a blue one. Driving home, I was not only trying to focus on the objective, simply proving they were there as well as the process of elimination it would take to scrutinize if any data recovered could have a source other than Sasquatch. I was going to initiate a technique that was so simple it almost seemed stupid. This was going to be the epitome of "low tech".

A few weeks later, the snow had melted in most areas and the ice was coming off the Clearwater River. I drove up to the river south of Clearwater Lake, just Southwest of Debs, MN about 15 miles. The water had flowed to it and it was fairly high but it wasn't so much flow that it would be difficult to paddle a kayak against. The access point I was at was rarely used and if it was it was used to travel down the Clearwater River, not up it. The clearings

I had mapped out were all within a mile of the river and ranged from 4 miles from the access point to 9 miles north to the furthest one. That night I loaded up my kayak and got things ready to leave early in the morning well before sunrise. I had to drive about an hour from my lake home to the access point. The next morning it was still dark when I left and drove to the river. I launched the kayak and paddled four miles upriver to the first clearing. After pulling up on shore I hiked the ½ mile back to the pinned location and located the area. I walked from the tree line into the grass and kicked the drop-kicked the ball. I then chased after it and picked it up and laughed at it. I threw it into the air a few times catching it and continued to laugh at it each time I looked at it. I placed it on the ground and kicked it soccer style and chased after it and kicked it again. I continued doing this while taking moments to laugh loudly at the ball. After about 30 minutes, I placed the ball in the dead grass which wasn't longer than 12 inches and took careful note of where in the clearing it was placed. I hiked back to the kayak and paddled downriver to my truck and left.

I had checked the forecast the night before and knew there would be minimal wind, under 5 mph, not strong enough to move the ball. I had also decided that if the ball was moved a short distance of under 15 feet, I couldn't rule out that a deer or bear had simply smelt the ball and nudged it around with its face. The ball would have to be moved a significant distance to have been done by a human or Sasquatch without the possibility of another animal being the source. If a bear tried to place almost any pressure at all on the ball with its paw, it would puncture. Canines may smell and nudge the ball too, but not likely to move it a long distance.

The purpose of my conduct with the ball and the playful interaction was simply to leverage the curiosity of a Sasquatch if one happened to be watching me from the tree line. I didn't do anything that seemed as if it could be construed as threatening. I didn't knock or call out. I didn't stand there and study the tree line. I went in, played with the ball, and left it.

The next morning, I drove back up to the river and paddled back to the area. I hiked into the clearing and noticed the ball was still in the exact same place I had left it. I picked it up and returned to the kayak and paddled upriver another mile to the area of the next pinpointed clearing. I hiked back to that location and repeated the process. I continued to do this over the next three days, taking the fourth off because of a high wind forecast in the area.

At this point I was questioning whether this process would produce any results as it was exhausting work with all the kayaking, waking up at 5AM, the hiking back and forth to the areas. On the day I arrived back upriver to the last of the six spots I had mapped, I repeated the process and placed the ball on the far end of the clearing which measured roughly 80 yards by 60 yards. The next morning I returned, and I immediately noticed the ball was not where I had left it. After scanning the area I spotted it on the far end of the open area, opposite of where I was standing. While walking over to it I paced it off and it had been moved roughly 70 yards with no wind overnight. It's important to note that even when there was a light 10 mph wind, it was almost unnoticeable in the clearing because of the height of the pines. They towered over the area at about 50 to 80 feet tall. The location was well protected from the wind.

I looked closely at the surfaces of the ball and noticed there were light, translucent-looking smears on it that appeared to be similar in texture to a very thin layer of tacky wax. I carried the ball back to the kayak and left the area, paddling about 8 ½ miles down the river back to the access. I had determined this would be the clearing I conducted any further research in, despite it being the most remote of the 6 I had mapped. In the week of traveling back and forth on the river, I never saw another human on land or on the river. This seemed to fit the bill as far as being secluded from human interaction. Even in the dog days of summer during the local tourist season that the lakes bring in, it should remain to be a non-traffic area. Even if someone did kayak or canoe down the river, the clearing was not visible from the waterway as it sat 3/4 mile to the northeast. The closest hiking trail was 4 miles away and the nearest roadway was almost 7 miles. The surrounding 3-mile radius was a such dense forest that it wouldn't be likely any human would be back in this area. It was difficult to walk through as you had to zigzag through the deadfall and timber.

14

FINE TUNING

I had met Doug Hajicek online and messaged him about the area, and the approach to researching it, and he seemed intrigued. Doug lived close to my area in Northern MN and was familiar with the general location of the clearing. This low-tech approach was different than what most were doing in the field. During our discussions we often talked about his upcoming Legend Meets Science 2 Documentary. One of the focus points of the Documentary was going to take advantage of the new technology and advancements in DNA testing and utilize a very controlled approach to evaluate suspected Sasquatch DNA. The discussion really made me realize that by leaving out all battery presence, and all technology from the field of research, if we created an environment that leveraged curiosity and never tried to interact in any way through vocalization or communication, maybe the area could be used to collect this DNA. Designing items that could be interacted with or moved, touched, etc. and in that process take trace evidence in hair samples, Sebum samples, and other DNA evidence.

Doug suspected that the Sebum could explain the waxy residue on the ball once it had been moved. Sebum is an oily, waxy substance produced by your body's sebaceous glands. Sebum is essential for pliable skin, but the levels of lipids secreted also contain skin cells. The secretion also offers antibacterial protection to small scrapes and cuts. Great Apes in captivity secrete so much of this it builds up into big waxy layers or clumps in the armpits, the inside of their elbows and the back of the knees. All primates utilize it to some degree. It would be likely that Sasquatch would too and would also explain some of the accounts of white or gray dried waxy prints left on car windows and different surfaces.

After discussing possible collection techniques, he suggested putting Velcro tabs on the ball. Placing a half dozen sticky-backed Velcro tabs on various areas of the ball may end up collecting a hair sample intertwined in the Velcro if the ball was picked up and carried.

The following week, I went out on a Thursday morning at sunup and went through the playful procedure of placing the ball in the field for about 45 minutes. I left the ball and returned the next day at sunup to see it had been moved again. This time about 50 yards into the tree line. While studying the Velcro tabs, I could see there were two hairs in one of the tabs which measured 8 and 10 inches long. The hairs were very fine and limp with a translucent appearance and coloration of bourbon and water. I had brought envelopes in the case and I had been lucky enough to find a hair sample. I also had sterile Q tips and envelopes for them to be able to collect a skin oil sample if there were any. I didn't notice any smears on the ball this time. I used sterile forceps to collect the hairs and noticed that the hairs didn't have much structural integrity to them, they just bent easily over almost from the tip of the forceps.

I was anxious to call Doug and tell him how the Velcro had worked. He became my sounding board when it came to the research. I would run theories or ideas by him, and he would offer his ideas and recommendations as well as play the skeptic to help vet the results. As the weeks went on, I decided to keep the same weekly routine. Deploy the objects I would leave on a Thursday Morning and retrieve them on Friday. I wasn't sure if this individual that was interacting with the ball habituated in the area or lived 30 miles away, but it was my intention to try to become part of its routine. If I made sure to always stick to the Thursday-Friday schedule, it could become comfortable with the fact that it always had a 24-hour window to explore the items and exercise its curiosity in them every week.

During the following 7 months, I stuck to that schedule. Each week would bring a new result as I changed up the items I would leave in the field. At times I was deploying 6 or 7 different items at once, all designed to collect DNA if they were interacted with. A few weeks into the research, I was having one of our hours-long messenger call meetings with Doug and we were discussing the idea of Sasquatch possibly being able to see in a UV vision spectrum. I had several years working with black lights, fluorescents, and UV perception in an industrial setting through some work I did with PPG industries. Doug had several years of bear research where he studied and filmed bears in hibernation. One thing he noticed was the number of blue items that were collected by the bears in their dens. Mainly trash, bottle caps, Dasani water bottles that they chewed on, plastic signs, and other blue items they drug into their den instead of leaving them lying in the open after chewing on them like they seemed to do with other colored items.

It was well established in science that Caribou see in a UV vision spectrum. Other pack herd animals were also documented to utilize a UV VS. Many breeds of dogs, deer, and other mammals were believed to see in it. And some theorize that perhaps at one time, humans did too but we simply evolved away from it. If bears could see in it, could Sasquatch? And if they did what would that look like? When we analyze certain things in nature in a UV spectrum, we notice that some subdued colors tend to be vivid and other bright colors tend to be subdued. In other words, perhaps colors we as humans describe as bright like yellow, orange and red aren't very bright in a UV Vision spectrum and other colors we would describe as subdued like Blue, Purple or Brown are actually brighter in a UV vision spectrum. Maybe this explains an affinity for blue items with bears.

Another interesting thing to consider is that many hard plastics contain a high amount of acrylic resin. It's the ingredient that makes plastic hard and durable. The more acrylic resin, the harder the plastic. Game cameras are made to be bear-proof and resist being chewed on and thus have a very high amount of acrylic resin in the plastic. Interestingly, the acrylic resin in its pure form has a fluorescent reflection under UV light. So does the UV coating on the eyeglasses we wear that are meant to filter out the sun's harmful rays. So does camera lenses. They all have a UV coating or film on them which likely reflects under UV light. What does this mean? If a Sasquatch can see in a UV Vision spectrum, your eyeglasses look like two fireflies in the dark across a field. The lens and possibly the plastic on a trail cam look to be glowing in the dark. Perhaps this is a reason why millions of game cams aren't capturing Sasquatch images?

The conversation led us to decide to correlate blue with many of the items we left. If I left a piece of Bit O Honey candy in a baby food jar, I would place it by a tree that had fluorescent blue flagging tape tied to its base. I left a boomerang that was painted fluorescent blue with Velcro tabs on the top and bottom of each end. I painted an entire game camera fluorescent blue and removed the batteries making it ineffective. All these items I left in the clearing on at least one visit and all of them were interacted with. The game cam I threw around in the field and then left it lay. I returned to find it hanging by its Velcro strap from a broken branch in a tree 30 yards away. The boomerang I threw a few times trying to display how it would return once thrown. I left it and something very interesting happened. It was gone. That was the only item out of dozens of items that I left over from the research project that wasn't returned. Perhaps it realized it was too useful as a tool for hunting that it simply kept it, I'm not sure.

I took small vials and filled them with water and a small pinch of blue glitter and capped them off. I carried these in my pocket each time I went into the area and left them here and there. When I noticed something had been moved from the trail, I accessed the clearing on like a dead limb or a rock, I would leave one of the small vials on the trail. I once found a tiny fishing bobber on the trail. There was no way a human had been walking back in the trees that far in this area since I had been there the day before and laid that there. I left a vial in return for the bobber. Each time I left a vial, it was taken when I returned. The vials looked like tiny snow globes when you shook them and shimmered in the sunlight. There's no way to eliminate the possibility of it being taken by an eagle or hawk or some other pack rat so I couldn't count on those interactions in any scientific way, but I always looked at the area they were taken from for prints or other signs that it could have been a Sasquatch.

15

SOMETHING SURREAL

I always wondered if whatever was interacting with the items, assuming it was a Sasquatch based on the interaction revealing what it was capable of and not capable of, do they wait until the middle of the night to explore and interact with the items? Or do they come out right after I leave? On week 8 of the project, I got the answer. It was a Thursday morning and I had pulled the kayak up on the shore of the river. I had left early that day and the sun still hadn't come up yet. I needed to be back in town by noon to meet a real estate client, so I was in a hurry and didn't want to break the protocol I had established by dropping by on Thursday and Picking up on Friday. Although I always brought my cell phone while kayaking in case I had an emergency, I didn't bring it into the area. I didn't bring any battery-powered devices into the area. Flashlights, GPS, Cameras, etc. I always left my phone in the kayak. I was wearing a backpack that had items I would leave that day; I had the ball under my arm as I walked along the same route I always used. There was a light trail starting to establish where I had walked over the past weeks.

About halfway to the clearing I was frozen in between steps as I heard a loud tree knock crack behind my back where my kayak was left. I stood staring at the ground and reminded myself what I had established for goals in this project. DO NOT look around and try to identify what made the sound. Just keep walking and act as if I hadn't heard it. Within two steps a second knock sounded off in front of me where the clearing was. It felt so surreal. They were here right now watching me. It's as if one had signaled that the guy in the kayak is here, and the other was responding that they could see me.

I had decided that any displayed vocalization, any knocks or clacks, any attempt they would portray to communicate with each other, I would ignore as if I didn't notice. I would not look around at the tree line or try to see if anything was around me. Just enter the site, play with the objects to leverage curiosity, and leave them. There was no way anything I did in the area could be perceived as a threat. I simply wouldn't acknowledge their presence. That was easier to do on paper than it was to do when you are in the dark and one is behind you and one in front of you. But I followed through and walked into the clearing, the sun was revealing all the forest's features and I played with the ball until it was well-lit. I left other items amongst the tree line with the flagging tape, and I returned to the kayak.

The following morning, I was kayaking up the river to the area. The sun was just starting to come up but it was still very dim. About halfway there I heard a knock come from the west side of the river about a hundred yards in front of me. I paddled quickly and closed the distance until I felt I was about in line with its location and there was another knock on the east side of the river a few hundred yards in front of me. I quickly paddled that distance and again, another knock on the west side in front of me. It was as if they were escorting me into the location. I reached the location and walked into the area and retrieved the items. The ball had been moved like it usually was. Lids were removed from jars I had left with a polished rock in one jar and a piece of Bit O Honey candy in the other. One of the jars was not only empty, but it also had the lid screwed back on. I noticed the smears on the jar and lid and quickly took a swab and placed it in the envelope. The ball also had another hair on it. When I retrieved all the items and prepared them for transport back, I returned to the kayak.

I stood at the tree line looking at my kayak and immediately noticed something out of place. The paddle had been disjointed at the midsection where the plunger button was, and half of the paddle was laying in the cockpit of the kayak and the other half was leaning against it. As I got closer, I noticed that my life jacket was on the seat but upside down from how I left it. The buckles which I always leave unclasped when I remove them were now clipped together. I stood there examining the kayak and shoreline. The shore where I had beached the kayak at the river's edge was like a river rock. However, just 20 feet down the river bank the shore was very fine black sand. Had I beached it there, I would likely have a footprint or two to examine. Or maybe it wouldn't have approached the kayak at all because of the sand and its ability to show a track. Regardless, I decided to make sure I beached the kayak in the sand area every time I returned to the location from here on out. It's a good example of how this project was a learn on the fly endeavor.

By the end of the 7 months, I had managed to collect 27 hair samples and 14 Sebum samples. I had heard dozens of knocks and different whistles. At one point I had knocks coming from four different locations within minutes of each other. The samples are being stored to be tested by DNA labs and hopefully, the results will be featured in a documentary along with results from samples across North America.

16

THE ULTIMATE DECEPTION

One element I had added to the project didn't turn out as I had anticipated. In research, we consider the evidence as it would pertain to Sasquatch to fall into one of four categories. Video/Images, DNA, castings, or audio recordings. Rarely is more than one collected from the same sight. One of the unique things about the Paterson/Gimlin film was that they had three of the four and had they known about DNA analysis back then, they likely could have had all four. They had the film of course. But they also knew exactly where she had stepped and had a trackway. They also had audio of their own interaction but none of the creature vocalizing. Had they known about DNA they could have looked at every track and every branch it may have touched and likely found a hair sample.

If we successfully collected DNA over seven months AND could have gotten an image or video, that would have been something very special to this project. Doug and I both felt that since I had created an environment in which it obviously felt comfortable enough to interact with items and didn't seem to perceive me as any sort of threat to keep it from expressing its curiosity about the items I left, maybe we could leverage that "trust" and catch it with its ass out. If on the last week, that ball wasn't a rubber ball but rather a foam 15" sphere with four lipstick 4K color and IR cameras with their own battery source all embedded in the foam core and then plastic dipped the ball to appear to be the ball they had always approached, could it be fooled? Perhaps it would approach the ball and at some point sense either a battery presence or IR presence and stop and turn away, it may be too late and be on video. If we left powered audio recorders on that last deployment of items in different areas of the tree line, could we catch it making audible interaction? It certainly wouldn't expect it after seven months of any of that ever being in the area. Is it possible to create such a comfortable and trustworthy setting that I could deceive it? If it didn't work, we would already have the DNA evidence we had collected up to that point. Why not give it a try.

In retrospect, we had already made a few fatal flaws. Although I never gave out the location of the research area, I did share the techniques we had developed and how we were trying to take a different approach to research. I had spoken openly about those efforts and given updates on several different YouTube channels in interviews. Every few weeks I shared our progress and success in collecting samples. Our plan is to have them tested in the labs. People knew I had the Lakehouse in the Park Rapids/Bemidji area. They knew I was working in the Pine Island Forest. I didn't see these updates as an issue since I wasn't sharing exact locations. The Pine Island Forest is hundreds of thousands of acres. I never referred to the river by name. Any pictures I shared were up close shots of the ball with hair samples in it and items I would leave in the field, not anything that revealed a background that would be identifiable. Nothing revealing the exact area was ever shared publicly. However, hundreds of emails and messages between Doug and I did disclose these details.

The week prior to what we referred to as the "ultimate deception", I kayaked into the area. It was very late in the fall and the air temps were in the 40s. As I pulled the kayak onto the shore and grabbed my backpack with the items for the last normal deployment, I immediately noticed the smell of ammonia. As I walked back to the clearing, I could smell it getting stronger. Once in the clearing, I walked the entire perimeter and the grass smelled like it had just been sprayed with fertilizer. I developed a headache from it after a few minutes. I left the ball out there after kicking it a few times and I walked around pulling tufts of grass out in different areas and shoving them into my backpack. I placed the grass samples into bags and saved them for analysis hoping the labs could identify the source.

It seemed impossible that the entire clearing could have been sprayed with something like this. It didn't seem to fit any natural explanation as to why the smell would be there. There were no agricultural fields in the area. Occasionally you would see state or federal efforts to control growth in certain areas using chemicals, but it didn't seem likely this late in the fall. On the paddle out, I stopped at two of the other clearings I had originally mapped as target areas I had explored and neither of the two areas had the smell. The next day I returned to the same smell and an unmoved ball. Up to this point, there were only five times that the ball hadn't been moved in seven months of weekly deployment.

There were other events that had occurred during the last four weeks of the project that on their own seemed odd. On their own, each event didn't raise any serious red flags, but collectively they were concerning. First, I had two males in their late 30's or early 40's parked on the private road that led to my lake house. There were only three homes on this road, and it wasn't a through street that led anywhere. I had seen them parked there in the late afternoon of a Wednesday when I had traveled from South Dakota to the lake house and was just arriving when I noticed the White Suburban. I called my neighbor whom I was very close friends with and trusted with the details of my research. He was a veteran who had served when I did. I asked him if he noticed the vehicle and he said it was there yesterday for a couple hours too. He had tried to approach it yesterday and it had drove away. At the time I had called him, he was not home and hadn't noticed it was back. I was going to walk over to it. I had already backed into my garage and hooked up my trailer and loaded the kayak for the next morning's trip up the river. As I walked halfway up my driveway they drove out and as they passed me the passenger was holding up a phone to photo or video me. It was odd.

The week following, I had my FLIR C5 in the kayak with me on Thursday and I had my iPad in a waterproof case on a Ram mount on the front of my kayak. It was connected to my C5 so I could hold the cell phone-sized FLIR in any direction and see the image displayed on the IPad without turning my head in any direction. I thought I heard a humming sound for a few minutes while starting up the river and finally held the FLIR up above my head at the sky where I felt the sound was coming from and the IPad image was revealing a heat source that appeared to be a battery and a drone. Within a mile or two of traveling the river, I couldn't see it anymore. Why would a drone be out at 6AM over this remote river and where would someone be operating it from? I didn't see any vehicles the last 15 miles of my trip to the river or parked in the areas around where I launched at. After visiting the site and leaving the ball and other objects as usual without anything further being out of the ordinary, I returned to my Vehicle.

On the way back home, I called Doug and told him about the

drone. His reply caught me off guard. He said the other night, on the nine live cams he has deployed at another site in Northern MN, he thought he saw a drone flying in front of one of the cameras. At this point, I shared with him about the guy who took my picture in my driveway and we both were puzzled and not sure what to make of it. I asked Doug if he thought I should keep going into the area as I was supposed to return to pick up the items the next morning. He said, "Why wouldn't you? It's not like we're doing anything illegal. It's public land, we aren't breaking any laws."

He was right. Why should we be concerned? I visited with my neighbor that evening. He had spent several years following his military service as a security contractor in Jordan. He had extensive experience with surveillance, night vision, FLIR Technology, etc. He agreed to come with me the following morning in his own vehicle and park several miles short of the launch area. He would arrive at the location and hike into a position in the tree line where he could see the launch area and the first mile up the river before it bends out of sight. He brought his FLIR with him and watched me kayak up the river, He called me on my phone and said the drone was back and directly above me about 400 to 500 feet. He watched me until I was out of his sightline. He had driven around all of the back roads surrounding the area, most of which were about 7 to 10 miles from the area I was kayaking, and saw no sign of vehicles or people.

The last event that occurred was the most puzzling. That week I had driven my GMC Yukon to the lake house instead of my truck. I hooked up my trailer as usual and loaded the kayak on Wednesday night. It was a very normal routine for me by this point. I left early in the morning on Thursday and drove to the launch site. I paddled up the river and deployed the items. I noticed nothing on the FLIR C5/IPad combo. After deploying the ball and other items, I paddled back to my Yukon and when I was a mile away, I immediately notice my trailer is not with my Yukon. I walk up the embankment to my vehicle and look closer. It's gone. I immediately thought that it had been stolen.

I did not use a lock on the trailer coupling and it wouldn't be hard for someone to simply unhook it, rotate it 90 degrees by hand and hook it up to their vehicle. I couldn't load my 12' kayak into my Yukon. I called my neighbor who knew where I was and told him what had happened. He said he would drive his truck to the launch site and we could put my kayak in his truck and he would follow me back to my place. I was going to call the sheriff to file a report. I took off my heavy jacket and my boots and put my sneakers on and my phone rang. It's my neighbor telling me, "Dude, your trailer is in your driveway." In my driveway?!? He said, "it's backed not my driveway." He asked if he should hook it up to come to the launch and I told him "No, just bring your truck." I wanted to see this for myself. When he showed up an hour later, he was laughing at me asking me if I was sure I had brought my trailer with me to the launch. I told him, how the hell would I get this 12' kayak here in my Yukon Denali, it wasn't a Yukon XL. I always took the trailer.

We returned to my house, and we examined the trailer. The license plate had been removed and the bolts holding the plate on were finger-tightened back into the holes. WTH is going on here? We spent the better part of an hour crawling around under the trailer to see if there had been some sort of tracking device placed on it. We found nothing. Why would someone take my trailer from my vehicle an hour from my home and return it to my home by backing it into my driveway and taking the license plate off it? They would have to know me, and where I lived. What would be the motive other than a practical joke?

I shared these strange events with others on my YouTube

channel and many thought I was losing my mind. They kept asking me if I was proclaiming there was some sort of conspiracy going on. Did the Govt take my trailer and fly a drone over me etc. I'm not saying any of that because I have no idea. I'm only sharing with you what happened. I offer no explanation and to this day, I still have no explanation. When you combine the events into one short four-week time frame and add them all together, it seems awfully suspicious. And yet, I have no explanation. It would have been interesting to see what kind of outcome we would have achieved with the cameras and audio recorders in the research area had they not been contaminated. But regardless, we did achieve the results we had hoped for by taking a research approach that was out of the box and trying something different.

17

DEVELOPED THEORIES

O ver the past few years of research, talking to other researchers, hearing thousands of encounters, investigating different encounter sites, talking to skeptics, and infusing all of that with four decades of remote outdoor guide experience, I've developed a few theories along the way. When I discuss these theories in interviews or on podcasts, I am very careful to make sure they are both presented and received with the understanding that I present them simply as theories and not facts. When anyone tries to present their theories or thoughts on Sasquatch as fact, that should be an immediate red flag. We operate in the arena of proving this mystery as true with very few facts. Some would argue there aren't any facts.

When I develop a theory, it is developed by utilizing a process of elimination that starts with coming up with any reasonable explanation for whatever result, trend, data, or proclamation we are examining. The goal being a search for an explanation that we can deem as most plausible. If we have five reasonable explanations to consider, start by discounting the one or two that are least likely. To put it simply, you are attempting to unmuddy the water. Out of the remaining explanations, it will be easier to determine which would be most plausible.

In addressing each theory, I will start with the root question that usually starts the process.

Why do encounters vary in the description of physical attributes as well as demeanor?

This is a great question and I see it addressed with different opinions often but very seldom backed up with any reasonable explanation as to why the person holds the opinion. After watching over a hundred encounters shared with Larry Batson, the renown artist who is regularly featured on Bigfoot Odyssey who draws these physical depictions based on details shared by the experiencer, and after reading thousands of encounter descriptions, I've started to see a trend. Many of the descriptions from encounters in the extreme southern hot climates seem to involve shorter hair structures. Short hair on the top of the head, shorter and coarse hair described on the body. Whereas extreme northern climates involve longer fine hair on the top of the head and body. Often it is described as flowing or hanging down from the arms and other areas of the body and head. I'm not referring to the middle of North America in the areas where winter is cold but not stupid cold or the areas where it gets hot but not year-round hot.

Let's consider areas like Arizona, Texas, and Florida to be extreme southern climates where heat is an issue and cold isn't as much of a factor. And let's consider areas of Canada, Montana, Wyoming, Idaho, Ohio, Michigan, and some of the Northeastern States like New Hampshire, Vermont, New York, and Pennsylvania to be the northern climates where cold can be a very real threat to one's ability to survive. All the areas in the middle like Tennessee, Missouri, the Carolinas, Virginia, etc., let's leave out of the discussion for now. In very northern climates where it gets down to zero to 50 below zero in the winter for four to six months a year, it makes sense to have a hair structure that would be more particles per square inch, longer in length, and fine rather than course to lay against the skin and serve as an insulating factor. Areas of extreme heat would require a hair structure that is coarser and stand up off the skin slightly, fewer particles per square inch, and shorter in length to serve as a ventilating factor. I'm not saying there couldn't be exceptions to the theory, but there is enough difference in the descriptions to explain this as a plausible explanation. The areas we withdrew from the discussion could see a blend of these traits because the climate isn't extreme enough one way or the other to require an overall adaption.

This extreme climate differential could also explain why there is a noticeable size discrepancy in many of the encounters in different regions. We see this in other species. White-tail deer for example are distinctly different in size depending on the area. In Alabama and Georgia, a 7-year-old Whitetail Buck at full maturity hardly weighs over 200 pounds. Whereas in Kansas, the Dakotas, Minnesota, Ohio, and other areas in the north, they will reach almost a 30% bigger body mass than the same species in other areas. The forage has a lot to do with it, but also the need for body mass to endure long cold winters. The caloric burn and metabolic rate in which it exists is much higher to survive in extremely cold climates. It is plausible to assume this could be true for Sasquatch. Physical descriptions in these Northern Climates often involve heights of 10" and body mass of upwards of 1,000 to 1,200 lbs. Physical descriptions in extremely hot southern climates will often not exceed 8' and the body mass is rarely more than 700 to 800 lbs.

Does all of this make this theory or opinion a fact? No. It is simply what I would consider a plausible explanation.

Why aren't there Sasquatch bones or skeletal remains found?

This is also a great question and a fair question. I often hear explanations ranging from decomposition acceleration on the forest floor, to "Do you ever see Mt Lion or bear skeletons?". I don't consider these to be plausible explanations although they are points to consider. After considering all the possible explanations, I think the most plausible one may be simpler than we expect it to be.

If Sasquatch all share the same common goal of remaining elusive and undisturbed by humans and other apex predators, then they likely establish clans that work as a family unit. Some have the role of sentinel, some may be the hunter, some may bear the responsibility of keeping juveniles safe, etc. Each likely has a place and a role. They work together and they NEED each other to accomplish the goal of remaining elusive. If they have a need for each other, they could very likely hold reverence for each other much like we as humans do. And if they hold reverence for each other, it is likely they may grieve the loss of one of their own. So much so that they simply bury them out of respect or to make sure their body isn't desecrated by other animals or found by humans. It's no different than we do for each other when we suffer the loss of someone we feel we needed. I think that explanation is more plausible than "they simply decompose really fast."

What is the biggest threat to Sasquatch when it comes to apex predators?

This question is going to invoke different opinions depending on where they are located. Obviously, without a doubt, man is the biggest threat to Sasquatch remaining elusive and unbothered. But when it comes to other threats in the wild, I would argue that in Florida there are many animals to fear in the swamps. Poisonous snakes and Alligators to name a couple. I spend most of my time in the Northern MN area, Wyoming, Montana Idaho, Michigan, and Wisconsin as well as most of the Canadian Provinces in central and western Canada when hunting and enjoying the outdoors. The discussion takes a different turn in those areas. Many would say Grizzly Bears or Polar Bears. I'm not sure that is the case. I think most of the time, an encounter involving a Sasquatch and an equal size and height Grizzly would most likely end in mutual respect for what each other is capable of. Most often when you see a Grizzly that size, it is alone.

If that is not often the case with Sasquatch, why would a Grizzly feel inclined to confront one? Also true with Mt Lions, they are most often alone, not in packs. But there is one animal that is almost never alone and tends to hunt in large packs. Wolves. Imagine that you are ten foot tall, 1,200 lbs of badass Sasquatch, and suddenly you are being confronted by a pack of 10 to 30 wolves, hunting together, and weighing up to 200 lbs of teeth and attitude. That is a serious threat that would be very hard to outrun or outfight. Fight or flight, neither option ends well with a large pack of wolves. When weighing all factors, I feel that trying to defend yourself against that threat would require several Sasquatch working in coordination to fend off a pack of Wolves. This may also support the seemingly evident reports of larger clan sizes in the northern territories where Wolves exist versus the smaller clan sizes in the southern states where they don't.

18

WHAT WILL IT TAKE?

When I take a step back and look at where this mystery has taken us and the road ahead, I can't help but wonder what is it going to take to prove to the world that there is an undiscovered, bipedal hominid that presently exists in this world? A body? I don't think there needs to be a body to show that it's out there.

I was reading an article on eLife, a site that features scientific research and published papers, titled "Single mosquito metatranscriptomics identifies vectors, emerging pathogens and reservoirs in one essay". Admittingly, it took me a bit to get through it as I do not hold a degree in anthropology or vector science. The article was about a project done by Joshua Batson, Gytis Dudas, Eric Haas-Stapleton, Amy L Kistler a corresponding author, Lucy M Li, Phoenix Logan, Kalani Ratnasiri, and Hanna Retallack. They represented a collaborative effort by Chan Zuckerberg Biohub, United States; Gothenburg Global Biodiversity Centre, Sweden; Alameda County Mosquito Abatement District, United States; Program in Immunology, Stanford University School of Medicine,

United States; Department of Biochemistry and Biophysics, University of California San Francisco, United States. Needless to say, this was a team of individuals whose expertise went beyond dabbling in DNA.

The project was done from 2017-2018. They were studying the transfer of viruses among vertebrae mammals and avian species by mosquitos (vectors). I'll do my best to simplify what their efforts entailed and the findings. They wanted to determine whether mosquitos were transferring viruses by feeding on a blood host and carrying any known viruses to the next individual on the menu. Those are my words, here are theirs.

"Mosquitoes are major infectious disease-carrying vectors. Assessment of current and future risks associated with the mosquito population requires knowledge of the full repertoire of pathogens they carry, including novel viruses, as well as their blood meal sources. Unbiased metatranscriptomic sequencing of individual mosquitoes offers a straightforward, rapid, and quantitative means to acquire this information. Here, we profile 148 diverse wild-caught mosquitoes collected in California and detect sequences from eukaryotes, prokaryotes, 24 known and 46 novel viral species. Importantly, sequencing individuals greatly enhanced the value of the biological information obtained. It allowed us to (a) speciate host mosquito, (b) compute the prevalence of each microbe and recognize a high frequency of viral co-infections, (c) associate animal pathogens with specific blood meal sources, and (d) apply simple co-occurrence methods to recover previously undetected components of highly prevalent segmented viruses. In the context of emerging diseases, where knowledge about vectors, pathogens, and reservoirs is lacking, the approaches described here can provide actionable information for public health surveillance and intervention decisions.

Mosquitoes are known to carry more than 20 different eukaryotic, prokaryotic, and viral agents that are pathogenic to humans (WHO,

2017). *Infections by these mosquito-borne pathogens account for over half a million human deaths per year.*

Female mosquitoes take up blood meals from humans and diverse animals in their environment and serve as a major source of trans-species introductions of infectious microbes. For well-studied mosquito-borne human pathogens such as West Nile virus, an understanding of the transmission dynamics between animal reservoir, mosquito vector, and human hosts has been essential for public health monitoring and intervention (Hofmeister, 2011)."

That was several mouthfuls. In their project, they set mosquito traps that caught live mosquitos overnight in two locations of wetlands in California. They determined there were four species of mosquitos in the area. Step one was identifying the genomic makeup of the four. They looked closely at each mosquito caught and identified the species and if it had fed on a blood host within the last 24 hours, it would be tested. Each mosquito was separately blended up into a tiny mosquito milk-shake and meta-sequenced to determine the mosquito's DNA and the blood host's DNA. They ended up catching 60 mosquitos that were female and had taken a recent blood feeding. They successfully identified all blood hosts and categorized them. The hosts ranged from Mule Deer, Raccoons, Rabbits, Waterfowl, Cows, etc. out of the 60, 15 were determined to be a human host and those samples were discarded since the project was to focus on the virus transfer by vectors in non-human verte-brae. This is where my light bulb started to kick into strobe mode.

Below is a graph of the 45 samples that weren't from a human blood host and categorized as to their origin. I am also including pertinent notes detailing the parameters of the project. **Warning:** Lots of nerd language that may or may not be beyond some of our comprehension. But it should be included for those wanting to have a detailed understanding of the project and how it was conducted.

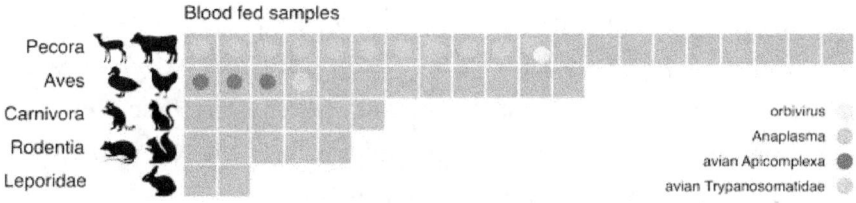

Mosquito Collection

"The 148 adult mosquitoes included in this study were collected at sites indicated in Figure 1—source data 1 using encephalitis virus survey (EVS) or gravid traps that were baited with CO_2 or hay-infused water, respectively. The collected mosquitoes were frozen using dry ice or paralyzed using triethyl amine and placed on a –15°C chill table or in a glass dish, respectively, for identification to species using a dissection microscope. Identified female mosquitoes were immediately frozen using dry ice in deep well 96-well plates and stored at –80°C or on dry ice until the nucleic acids were extracted for sequencing."

RNA preparation

"Individual mosquitoes were homogenized in bashing tubes with 200uL DNA/RNA Shield (Zymo Research Corp., Irvine, CA, USA) using a 5mm stainless steel bead and a TissueLyserII (Qiagen, Valencia, CA, USA) (2x1 min, rest on ice in between). Homogenates were centrifuged at 10,000xg for 5 min at 4°C, supernatants were removed and further centrifuged at 16,000xg for 2 min at 4°C after which the supernatants were completely exhausted in the nucleic acid extraction process. RNA and DNA were extracted from the mosquito supernatants using the ZR-DuetTM DNA/RNA MiniPrep kit (Zymo Research Corp., Irvine, CA,

USA) with a scaled down version of the manufacturer's protocol with Dnase treatment of RNA using either the kit's DNase or the Qiagen RNase-Free DNase Set (Qiagen, Valencia, CA, USA). Water controls were performed with each extraction batch. Quantitation and quality assessment of RNA was done by the Invitrogen Qubit 3.0 Fluorometer using the Qubit RNA HS Assay Kit (ThermoFisher Scientific, Carlsbad, CA, USA) and the Agilent 2100 BioAnalyzer with the RNA 6000 Pico Kit (Agilent Technologies, Santa Clara, CA, USA)."

Library prep and sequencing

"Up to 200 ng of RNA per mosquito, or 4 µL aliquots of water controls extracted in parallel with mosquitoes, were used as input into the library preparation. A 25 pg aliquot of External RNA Controls Consortium (ERCC) RNA Spike-In Mix (Ambion, ThermoFisher Scientific, Carlsbad, CA, USA) was added to each sample. The NEBNext Directional RNA Library Prep Kit (Purified mRNA or rRNA Depleted RNA protocol; New England BioLabs, Beverly, MA, USA) and TruSeq Index PCR Primer barcodes (Illumina, San Diego, CA, USA) were used to prepare and index each individual library. The quality and quantity of resulting individual and pooled mNGS libraries were assessed via electrophoresis with the High Sensitivity NGS Fragment Analysis Kit on a Fragment Analyzer (Advanced Analytical Technologies, Inc), the High-Sensitivity DNA Kit on the Agilent Bioanalyzer (Agilent Technologies, Santa Clara, CA, USA), and via real-time quantitative polymerase chain reaction (qPCR) with the KAPA Library Quantification Kit (Kapa Biosystems, Wilmington, MA, USA). Final library pools were spiked with a non-indexed PhiX control library (Illumina, San Diego, CA, USA). Pair-end sequencing (2 × 150 bp) was performed using an Illumina NovaSeq or NextSeq sequencing system (Illumina, San Diego, CA, USA). The pipeline used to separate the sequencing output into 150-base-pair pair-end read FASTQ files by library and to load files onto an

Amazon Web Service (AWS) S3 bucket is available on GitHub at https:// github.com/czbiohub/utilities."

Mosquito species validation

"To validate and correct the visual assignment of mosquito species, we estimated SNP distances between each pair of mosquito transcriptomes by applying SKA (Split Kmer Analysis) (Harris, 2018) to the raw fastq files for each sample. The hierarchical clustering of samples based on the resulting distances was largely consistent with the visual assignments, with each cluster containing a majority of a single species. To correct likely errors in the visual assignment, samples were reassigned to the majority species in their cluster, resulting in 7 changes out of 148 samples and one species assignment for a sample lacking a visual assignment."

Host and quality filtering

"Raw sequencing reads were host- and quality-filtered and assembled using the IDseq (v3.2) (Kalantar et al., 2020) platform https://idseq.net, a cloud-based, open-source bioinformatics platform designed for detection of microbes from metagenomic data."

Blood meal calling

"For each of the 60 blood fed mosquito samples from Alameda County, we selected each contig with LCA in the subphylum Vertebrata, excluding those contained in the order Primates (because of the possibility of contamination with human DNA). For each sample, we identified the lowest rank taxonomic group compatible with the LCAs of the selected contigs. (A taxonomic group is compatible with a set of taxonomic groups if it is an ancestor or descendent of each group in the set.)

For 44 of the 45 samples containing vertebrate contigs, this rank is at class or below; for 12 samples, it is at the species level. Each taxonomic assignment falls into one of the following categories: Pecora, Aves, Carnivora, Rodentia, Leporidae. In Figure 5, each sample with a blood meal detected is displayed according to which of those categories it belongs (Underlying data for Figure 5 are provided in Supplemental Data file bloodmeal_calls.tsv, with microbe categories tested for each sample summarized in samples_taxa.csv). The remaining sample, CMS001_022_Ra_S6, contained three contigs mapping to members of Pecora and a single contig with LCA Euarchontoglires, a superorder of mammals including primates and rodents; we annotate this sample as containing Pecora.

Notably, 19 samples contain at least one contig with LCA in genus Odocoileus and another contig with LCA genus Bos. While the lowest rank compatible taxonomic group is the infraorder Pecora, it is likely that a single species endemic in the sampled area is responsible for all of these sequences. Given the observational data in the region (described in the main text), that species is likely a member of Odocoileus whose genome diverges somewhat from the reference."

19

WHAT COULD WE LEARN FROM THE
PROJECTS?

Whaht if they had done this study in a remote part of
Alaska, British Columbia, Idaho, etc. where humans
were unlikely to be? They had determined that even with strong
wind patterns, an average mosquito couldn't travel more than 20
miles in its short life cycle. I've been in remote areas where I know
there were likely a very small number of humans in that range if
any. And, what if they threw out all the vertebrae mammal blood
hosts and only looked at the ones that showed a part human/un-
known primate DNA sequence? Maybe you'd have to catch a thousand mosquitos before you found one that fed on a Sasquatch
rather than a deer, moose, bear, etc. Or maybe you'd find a dozen.
Who knows?

It occurred to me that the cost of testing that many samples
were going to be expensive if done without any partnership with a
university lab or grant funding. But technology is advancing
extremely fast in DNA technology by ten-fold annually.

Shortly after reading this, I found another paper written on a
project where two scientists were researching and discovering new

species of butterflies. This project was done more recently and a lab they had partnered with had created a handheld sequencer the size of a cell phone. It did not contain a library of sequenced DNA samples of every living organism on earth since they wouldn't need a library that vast for the project they were doing. It simply held all the library of samples of insects in the area they were exploring. It was a fraction of the entire known library and thus could compute faster. The device had a probe on it that when touched to a butterfly's wing, it would sequence the insect's DNA and compare it to the library. Each insect took about two hours to compute and show a result. They ended up discovering two new species within a few months.

Again, I found myself wondering...What if they had loaded that device with known vertebrae mammals and avian species in one given remote area and you set your mosquito traps. Could the device accomplish the same task?

I contacted three individuals who had been part of that vector study. I did not lead off with, "My names is Jeff and I'm trying to prove that Bigfoot exists..." I didn't want to get hung up on in the first 10 seconds. I simply asked about the capability of the technology. Asking if it could be repeated to unveil results that would show results pertaining to humans instead of other vertebrae mammals? One interesting point they made was that there is a line you must be careful not to cross. And it's an impor-tant ethical line. If you had the human result of a blood host and you sequenced it, you now could identify who it is as well as what diseases they may have (HIV, Covid, etc.). And that could violate their right to privacy in those matters. It was a very valid point. But, yes, it could be done. Not only could it be done, but the technology was there to make it a portable device to test in the field.

After spending a 37-week stint attempting to collect hair

samples by paddling over a thousand miles, this sounded like a much simpler way to get far greater results.

My hope is to organize a collaborative effort with a university that may have an interest in putting a thumbs up or thumbs definitively to the Sasquatch mystery. Through the efforts of deploying mosquito traps over the course of one prime mosquito season in several remote areas across remote areas of North America, and collecting thousands of samples to be tested, could you identify an unknown primate sequence that existed in multiple geographical areas, and they all matched each other as the SAME unknown species with an identical genomic imprint? Wouldn't this be faster than collecting hairs, snot, and turds from animals all over the place? I think it would be and I believe that it's possible to implement.

The reason it would be possible isn't just because of advanced technology, it's because it would involve those outside of the bigfoot community. We as a community are standing in the corner of a room and seem to be relying on each other to find answers. We assume that those outside of the group of believers wouldn't be willing to risk their career and reputation being involved in such a project. I don't believe that to be true. Maybe some wouldn't want to be involved, but if it was a project where all they had to do is implement and test the samples you provide, you aren't asking for their opinion. You are simply asking for the results. And being a part of putting a conclusive thumbs up or down to this issue is something they wouldn't mind being a part of.

This is going to be my focus moving into 2023/2024. It won't be easy and there will need to be a lot of relationships and partnerships built, but I am determined to try. Short of trying to harvest one, I can't think of any other effort that may hold the potential of moving this ball downfield more than this one. Videos, pictures, audio samples, castings, where have they gotten us? I'd argue that in the 50-plus years since the Patterson/Gimlin film, it hasn't gotten us very far. However, with advancing technology combined with the efforts of so many citizen scientists out in the field working together, I believe that we can change that. We need to look beyond the corner of the room we find ourselves in for help. Let's invite those who are professionals in different areas of science to join us. Stop assuming they will say no. Often times it's not the event someone finds unappealing, it's the invite. Thousands of encounters aren't a coincidence, they are a collective testimony that something is out there and we need the help of those in the scientific community to come alongside us to put this matter to rest.

A SINCERE THANK YOU

I want to end this writing endeavor by saying thank you to all of those who have been there on this journey. First and foremost, Doug Hajicek for making me realize that carrying around the burden of having an encounter and never finding someone to talk about it with is unhealthy. Sharing it with others is not only healthy for your own mental state but it is helpful and assuring to those who have had encounters and fear talking about it to anyone. Doug's help throughout my research was invaluable. He was a voice of reason when I couldn't find a reasonable explanation or option. Thank you!

Also, I want to thank those who have been there throughout my experience of educating myself on the subject and learning valuable information from trusted sources. People like Doug, Blaine and Alex Hijacek, Leon Thompson, Joe Snyder, Steve Kulls, Dr. Russ Jones, Pat Turner, Russell Van Zilen, Matt Larson, Aleks Petakov, Brent Dill, Max Powers, and the hundreds of others who have been an influence on me.

Most of all, I want to thank my father for teaching me about the outdoors. You introduced me to all of the passions the wilderness has to offer, and you did so in a way that taught me not to be afraid of what I may encounter. It's a legacy I have tried to uphold in the teaching of my own sons and I've tried to do it in a way that honors the way you did it for me. Thank you, dad.

AFTERWORD

Go to hangarıpublishing.com to learn more about the Author and stay up to date with their newest releases.

www.ingramcontent.com/pod-product-compliance
Lightning Source LLC
Chambersburg PA
CBHW071211120626
46546CB00006B/2508